Composition and Cornel West

COMPOSITION AND CORNEL WEST

Notes toward a Deep Democracy

KEITH GILYARD

Southern Illinois University Press / Carbondale

11 10 09 08   4 3 2 1

Library of Congress Cataloging-in-Publication Data
Gilyard, Keith, 1952–
  Composition and Cornel West : notes toward a
deep democracy / Keith Gilyard.
      p. cm.
  Includes bibliographical references and index.
  ISBN-13: 978-0-8093-2854-3 (alk. paper)
  ISBN-10: 0-8093-2854-2 (alk. paper)
1. African Americans—Intellectual life. 2. African
American philosophy. 3. West, Cornel—Philosophy.
4. West, Cornel—Political and social views.
5. Democracy—United States. 6. Rhetoric—
Philosophy. 7. Rhetoric—Political aspects—United
States. 8. Rhetoric—Social aspects—United States.
9. English language—United States—Rhetoric.
I. Title.

E185.86.G495 2008
305.896'073—dc22   2007033416

Printed on recycled paper. ♻
The paper used in this publication meets the minimum
requirements of American National Standard for Information Sciences—Permanence of Paper for Printed
Library Materials, ANSI Z39.48-1992. ⊗

In memory of
Nefertiti Nicole Williams
(1986–2006)
outstanding and beautiful journalist

I give much weight to teaching in the academy and in the larger society. In fact, the priority I give to reading and speaking is closely related to the centrality of teaching in my intellectual vocation. In this sense, I am more a public teacher than public intellectual (a phrase I have never used to describe myself, though I have also never rejected it!), more interested in Socratic probing of the public than pronouncing blueprints for the public.

—Cornel West, "Philosophy and the Funk of Life"

If there is a master term in my text—and work—it is democracy.

—Cornel West, "The Tragicomic and the Political in Christian Faith"

Contents

Acknowledgments   xi

1. Flight West   1
2. The Roots of a Deep-Democratic Project   7
3. Socratic Commitment and Critical Literacy   27
4. Tracking Prophetic Witness   52
5. Tragicomic Hope in Democracy   77
6. Landing Song 99

Notes   123
Bibliography   137
Index   153

Acknowledgments

EVEN MODEST projects have their communal aspects. I thank Cornel West again for helping to set me flowing on this particular initiative. I am also appreciative of his nonpareil assistant, Maryann Rodriguez, for handling my visit to Princeton University with generosity and grace. The remarkable students in my graduate seminar "The Rhetoric of bell hooks and Cornel West," which I co-taught with Elaine (Dr. E) Richardson, inspired my attempt to turn a shopworn story about a chance encounter on an airplane into something fresher and more rigorous. Karl Kageff insisted that I do so. He and the staff at Southern Illinois University Press have been first-rate from beginning to end. Stephen Schneider, Vorris Nunley, David Holmes, and Bradford T. Stull, all keen intellects and accomplished scholars, proved to be enthusiastic and most insightful manuscript reviewers. It is an open secret that I lack the ability to pull off everything they desired, but I hope they recognize the improvements they made possible. My career-long friend and mentor, Geneva Smitherman, provided clarity on a point or two. My indispensable brother, Andrew Vachss, accepted a draft of this project as a provocation to expound upon a number of issues in a way that has been most useful to me. This is a decades-old tradition. And upstart Kevin A. Browne, ace doctoral student and research assistant, deftly facilitated manuscript preparation and submission.

I wish to acknowledge my undergraduate students, especially Agnes Domboroczki and Lynsey Wittman, who granted permission for me to use excerpts in chapter 3 of their writing on literacy and on majority rule, respectively. Lastly, I thank Babygrande Records for permission to quote from the work of Jean Grae and Viper records for permission to reprint lyrics by Immortal Technique.

ACKNOWLEDGMENTS

1
Flight West

IN 1998, I settled onto a propeller plane heading from University Park Airport to Philadelphia. The passenger strapped in the window seat next to me was Cornel West, who had spoken the previous night at Penn State. Even before takeoff, he was already intently reading a book in preparation for an upcoming debate with the author to take place at Harvard University. He explained that he had to identify the author's ontological premises. Of course, I planned to interrupt his preparation and seize a private audience for about forty minutes with one of the most celebrated, important, and certainly controversial academics in America. But I intended nothing overly heavy, just two brothas kickin it away from the crowd. Aware of his devotion to Christian prophecy and of my own waffling agnosticism, I noted nervously when we hit an air pocket how quickly one can convert to religion at thirteen thousand feet. He laughingly affirmed my observation, gesturing with his arm and hand to suggest how, in his words, "All that secularity just flies out of the window."

At one point, he inquired as to my academic pursuits. "I do composition," I offered somewhat mischievously. I could just as easily have claimed rhetoric, which I imagine would have been more-familiar intellectual space for him, as he possesses, for example, no shortage of commentary about Socrates, Plato, and Foucault. I could have offered African American literature as a basis for conversation given how much he draws on the work of Ralph Ellison, James Baldwin, and Toni Morrison. Or I could have mentioned linguistics and played to his interest in Ludwig Wittgenstein—or education and spoken to his research on John Dewey. At this remove, I cannot be sure of all the reasons that I cast my disciplinary identity strictly in the field of composition, though I suspect that it had something to do with defiantly taking pride in a pursuit that is often undervalued. At the time, I was serving as assistant chair of the Conference on College Composition and Communication and planning the following year's annual convention to be held in Atlanta for thirty-five hundred members of the organization. I felt no need that day, or most days, to legitimate composition studies by linking it to more widely recognizable or prestigious discourse. I suppose that I was also testing his knowledge. (I have already confessed to mischief.) Did he consider writing instruction simply utilitarian? Or was composition not a learned topic at the level of the meditations on being from which I had distracted him? At any rate, no vibrant response followed, just a polite nod before we moved on to other ideas, including a peep into his appointment book and a very graciously extended dinner invitation that I have yet to cash in. More pressing to me have been memories of an ironic moment. West has had a tremendous impact of which he seemed largely unaware. Certainly he knew that folks taught composition but not the extent of our field's professionalizing—organizations, workshops, research forums, special interest groups, resolutions, lobbying efforts, policy statements, consultancies, degree programs, awards, journals, books. A beginning list of scholars in our field who have cited him include, along with myself, Min-Zhan Lu, Geneva Smitherman, Michelle Hall Kells, David Holmes, Tom Fox, Arnetha Ball, Ted Lardner, Gail Okawa, Richard Miller, Ilene Crawford, Deborah Mutnick, Richard Marback, Beth Daniell, Todd Destigter, Susan Kates, Karen Kopelson, Morris Young, Wendy Hesford, Bradford Stull, Carol Severino, Mary Soliday, Howard Tinberg, Carmen Kynard, Steven Mailloux, and, most extensively, Hephzibah Roskelly, Kate Ronald, Linda Flower, Elenore Long, and Lorraine Higgins.[1] Out of my reflections about this influence and West being seemingly oblivious to it, this project is born.

It is profoundly within the purview of composition studies to address the concerns raised by West about educating a critical citizenry who will promote democratic values and who will draw upon a heritage of what West terms a "deep democratic tradition" to fashion humane responses to unwarranted social misery (*Democracy Matters* 13). Composition can contribute primarily to what we may call a *deep democracy* by fostering critical inspections of language. Much of the daily interaction for all of us is instantiated through language; thus, language is a key analytic category for anyone proposing social change. Some declare such linguistic and discursive scrutiny to belong properly to the realm of rhetoric or discourse analysis or media studies, even literary criticism and cultural studies. I won't contest the point. In the interests not of legitimacy but of more interdisciplinary reach, I am embracing *rhetorical education* as an umbrella term to describe all examination of and instruction in the strategic uses of language in whichever disciplinary homes the activity occurs. Although I still employ the term *composition* in this text, I mean it in terms of this expanded definition. This usage also is connected to my awareness that composition can be a highly political term that extends beyond an association in the popular imagination that it is the mere teaching of writing techniques. Bradford T. Stull, for example, views composition as a "state of intentionality, a process of study" that one uses to compose, in essence, a life (5). He sees W. E. B. Du Bois, Martin Luther King Jr., and Malcolm X as "emancipatory compositionists" who employed multimodal literate practices to front the sociopolitical and agitate for social change (3). Du Bois, King, and Malcolm consumed, in Stull's words, "foundational theological and political language of the American experience" (3). But they did not consume uncritically and therefore questioned "this language and thus the American experience itself" (3).

We should wish such a life of engagement, without the tragic consequences, for all of our students. We should lead them to engage in critical reception and production of language rather than lethargically to reproduce the status quo. In some sense, we should agree that only perilously can the idea of a productive life in the polis be separated from ongoing scrutiny of the imperfections—whatever our take on these blemishes—of the American political and educational order. Composition, at one level, involves the learning and teaching of skills. But skills never operate neutrally, nor do skilling and drilling. Developing metaawareness about language, a way to assess its various deployments, including one's own, should be a crucial component, as I have long argued, of writing classrooms. We must at some point face squarely Stull's simple but potent query: "whom, what, does composition serve?" (1).

If composition and rhetorical education more broadly are to gain or retain momentum as a democratizing force, even in a college environment of corporate-culture encroachment, the emphasis on certification over inquiry, and the championing of private rights over public good, then they have to become or remain spaces in which to "take back higher education," as education theorists Henry Giroux and Susan Searls Giroux would put it. Concerned to make democracy substantive, as opposed to being simply procedural, the Girouxs understand higher education as a contested domain that yet offers conditions for (I think my good friends have rap aspirations) "resisting depoliticization" and "challenging the politics of accommodation that subjects education to the logic of privatization" (285). Furthermore, in their view, a progressive politics of higher education "refuses to define students as simply consuming subjects, and actively opposes the view of teaching as a market-driven practice and learning as a form of training" (285). At stake, they argue, is the future of higher education as well as "the nature of existing modes of democracy and the promise of an unrealized democracy—a democracy that promises a different future, one that is filled with hope and mediated by the reality of democratic-based struggles" (285).

Teachers and scholars of rhetorical education, to connect more with Girouxist optimism than with complacency and despair, should remember that possibilities for change imminently abound. Thousands upon thousands of students enroll in first-year writing courses every year. First-year writing is the course most taught in the American academy. Thousands more students enroll in additional courses in rhetorical education. These realities make rhetorical education a vital laboratory for democratic experimentation, an opportunity too serious to ignore. Or as West observes, "Universities, colleges, and some professional schools, though increasingly given over to hi-tech and computers, still provide one of the few institutional arenas in which serious conversation about new ideological space can take place in liberal capitalist democracies" (*American Evasion of Philosophy* 222).

It is in this vein that West's voice has helped to energize our field. In *Democracy Matters*, he continues to be troubled by what he perceives to be a widespread diminution of democratic spunk. He sees listlessness and resignation among the rank-and-file at the same time that business elites and the Christian Right pursue an imperialist agenda that emphasizes, in his words, "free-market fundamental-ism, aggressive militarism, and escalating authoritarianism" (3–7). Regarding enlightened leadership, he notes that it has been displaced by "elite salesmanship to the demos" (3). West does, however, take hope in youth activism such as the fervor that surrounded the 2004 presidential election. I think of my daughter who at the age of fif-teen peered with high anxiety at the television coverage in 2000 and could barely wait to stand in line with me four years later, which she exuberantly did at 7:30 A.M., to cast her first ballot for a presidential candidate. Regrettably, the pickings were slim, and she abhorred the election result. Yet, she and numerous others like her represent the exciting potential for democratic enactment, both inside and outside of the academy.

How do we cultivate such democratic nerve and verve? West urges us all to consult the work of great democratic public intellectuals, art-ists, and activists—Ralph Waldo Emerson, Lorraine Hansberry, Her-man Melville, Ida B. Wells-Barnett, Walt Whitman, Eugene O'Neil, John Coltrane, Frederick Douglass, and Ella Baker, to name a few. These figures have contributed significantly to keeping the American democratic project alive. In addition, West proposes the use of three particular discursive strategies. The first, Socratic commitment, is a relentless examination of received wisdom coupled with a willing-ness to adopt the role of a *parrhesiastes*, a frank or fearless speaker in confrontation with irresponsible power.[2] The second, prophetic witness, entails an abiding concern with justice and the plight of the less privileged. A prime imperative is to reduce social suffering. The third, tragicomic hope, is an indomitable, keep-on-pushing sensibility reflective of the African American freedom struggle, blues, and jazz. The hope, for West, is that these strategies lead to the formation of a democracy that is deep enough to accomplish several expansive aims, namely, "shore up international law and multilateral institutions that preclude imperial arrangements and colonial invasions," "promote wealth-sharing and wealth-producing activities among rich and poor nations abroad," and, generally, "facilitate the principled transfer of wealth from well-to-do to working and poor people by massive invest-ments in health care, education, and employment, and the preserva-tion of our environment" (*Democracy Matters* 62). In other words, the goal is to make power accountable with the practical resources at our disposal. The relationship between this quest and rhetorical education and how West has helped to animate the work of educators working with evolving student-citizens as part of an adventure that gestures toward deep democracy are what this monograph explores.

The following chapter sketches the development of West's thinking with respect to specific strands of philosophy, political science, religion, and cultural studies. The goal is to trace the formation of the style of criticism he calls prophetic pragmatism and to indicate how prophetic pragmatism now splinters into the categories Socratic commitment, prophetic witness, and tragicomic hope when West addresses a popular audience, as is his intent in *Democracy Matters*. Although some may think the material covered in my modest genealogy is distant from composition, I try to keep before readers the relationship between West's developing thought and rhetorical education. Chapters 3, 4, and 5 shift focus to concentrate on composition praxis, although the ideas of West frame those sections as well. In other words, how can we and how do we conceive of work in rhetorical education in relation to Socratic commitment (chapter 3), prophetic witness (chapter 4), and tragicomic hope (chapter 5)? The concluding section (chapter 6), with the aid of an in-person assist by West, considers the implications of how we have more or less answered the question. In addition, I comment on the prospects for rhetorical education relative to the continual quest for a deeper, more perfect democracy.

In a sense, this book is one of consciously aware imagination in that I am guessing at the content of a very long conversation that could unfold, though never could there be enough time to complete it, if West viewed rhetorical education as central to his work and his work as central to rhetorical education. I imagine, for example, that if he wrote a book on pedagogy, say *Teaching Matters*, it would be somewhat Freirean, maybe something along the lines of bell hooks's *Teaching to Transgress* and *Teaching Community*. But in the absence of that development, I have tried to make explicit his pedagogy—or at least his case for a particular pedagogy of composition. I imagine passengers conversing passionately about composition, Socratic commitment, prophetic witness, tragicomic hope, and deep democracy whether on the ground, sailing along, or roaming the skies.

2
The Roots of a Deep-Democratic Project

BEFORE CONSIDERING more explicitly the link between deep democracy and rhetorical education, it is helpful to trace the roots of the idea in the earlier writings of Cornel West so we can ascertain how he has come to promote the discursive strategies he dubs Socratic commitment, prophetic witness, and tragicomic hope. The themes were sounded as far back as 1982 in his first book *Prophesy Deliverance!* Over the ensuing years, these themes have been mostly encoded and articulated with respect to four strands of West's theorizing, namely, philosophical pragmatism, progressive Marxism, prophetic Christianity, and the tragicomic as related to African American humanism. Because I am interested in the evolution of West's thinking and rhetorical practice, I sometimes dispense with the convention of writing about his work in the present tense. Even what I refer to as "present" might already be somewhat "past" in a theoretical sense by the time these words appear in print, though I do not anticipate major ruptures or departures.

Pragmatism and Its Problems

In his debut book, West extols the virtues of an inquiring community, one that develops knowledge through continual dialogues that allow any previous truth claim to be called into question. In its rejection of foundations and absolute certainty, this ideal community reflects the tenets of pragmatism, the dominant strand of American philosophy. In this view, truth is not gained through deductive reasoning but by means of inductive experimentation and rigorous assessment. As John Dewey explained in "The Development of American Pragmatism," the focus is "not upon antecedent phenomena but upon consequent phenomena; not upon precedents but upon the possibilities of action" (quoted in the *Cornel West Reader*, 177).[1] Propositions are weighed by outcomes. Is this a good road to take? Only after the journey can we say for sure. This does not mean that some hypotheses are not more informed than others, just that certitude lies in experience. Therefore, pragmatism, in its empiricism, takes exception to Cartesian rationalism, or the concept that truth can be known only through specifiable principles of reason. Pragmatism holds suspect the search for philosophical foundations and binds philosophy to social and historical circumstances. It restlessly interrogates received and conventional wisdom.

When West first grappled extensively with pragmatism, he appropriated its insights with the aim of forging an African American critical method that was to be used to examine modern American life and set an agenda for African American political activism. By the appearance in 1989 of *The American Evasion of Philosophy*, his most elaborate written engagement with pragmatism, he advocated applicability beyond strictly African American concerns. He discerned in the tradition of pragmatism a major impulse to redress social wrong and a moral emphasis, which felt, and feels, important to him in a postmodern age: "I am convinced that the best of the American pragmatist tradition is the best America has to offer itself and the world" (8).

West recognized Ralph Waldo Emerson, who valued self-definition and people's perceptions, or *doxa*, over the presumed objectivity of philosophers' knowledge, or episteme, as the most important forerunner of American pragmatism. Attempting to free himself psychically from European cultural influence, though not achieving that desire wholly, Emerson prefigured scholars like Dewey by emphasizing individuality, optimism, experimentation, and amelioration. His style of cultural criticism directly influenced the first prominent American philosophers who came to be formally known as pragmatists, namely, Charles Sanders Peirce and William James.[2] Emerson did not refute the major currents of European philosophy in terms of philosophical discourse. As West described it, Emerson *evaded* that philosophy: "To evade modern philosophy means to strip the profession of philosophy of its pretense, disclose its affiliations with structures of powers (both rhetorical and political) rooted in the past, and enact intellectual practices, i.e., produce texts of various sorts and styles, that invigorate and unsettle one's culture and society" (*American Evasion of Philosophy* 37). Emerson's groundbreaking achievement was not unproblematic, however. Neither is the history of pragmatism. Despite his libertarian sentiments and various democratic actions, Emerson remained somewhat of an apologist for American expansionism and racism.[3] This dual legacy has informed certain expressions of pragmatism by the likes of intellectuals such as Sidney Hook, Reinhold Niebuhr, and Richard Rorty, since the nineteenth century.[4]

After Peirce formally inaugurated American pragmatism in the 1870s, and James secured increased popularity for its precepts beginning in the late 1890s, the school of thought, in West's analysis, reached its apotheosis in the work of Dewey and his democratic faith in common people. Dewey, West suggested, understood pragmatism as a "historical theory of critical intelligence and scientific inquiry and of reform and amelioration" (*American Evasion of Philosophy* 70). A guiding purpose for Dewey, therefore, was "to demystify and defend critical intelligence . . . to render it more and more serviceable for the enhancement of human individuality, that is, the promotion of human beings who better control their conditions and thereby more fully create themselves (i.e., advance creative democracy)" (*American Evasion of Philosophy* 72). Dewey's convictions stemmed largely from his observation of the nation's emerging industrialization, fledging monopoly capitalism, increasing immigrant waves, and widespread poverty. Most important, he viewed critical intelligence to be within the reach of all, which accounted for his emphasis on humanitarian efforts and educational initiatives during his visits to Jane Addams's Hull House and his tenures at the University of Chicago and Columbia University. Moreover, as West understood the matter, Dewey knew that "schools themselves were ideologically contested terrain, always worth fighting for and over" (85). Although the value of Dewey's work is undeniable and almost unassailable, West did criticize him for his gradualism and failure to articulate concrete plans for larger-scale social reform. Although Dewey was a self-described democratic socialist, he failed to employ, in West's view, a serious enough class analysis and conveniently confined his practical vision to schooling. He placed more hope in an ethical project of democracy than a political one.

Of course, Dewey's emphasis on education plays well with progressive composition instructors *in their role as instructors*. Like West, they may point to Dewey's shortcomings in wider realms, but they certainly concur that education, particularly of the dialogic sort that Dewey championed, is a crucial vehicle for social advancement. They believe that knowledge is co-constructed in their classrooms. Knowledge fashioned on previous occasions can be dispensed as information, but teachers and students must create new knowledge through inquiry and transaction. Even a student pursuing study independently is not being given knowledge; he or she is claiming it—in the process of becoming the model critical subject—through the active, transactional process that reading is. Although Deweyan methods no longer hold as much sway over American education in general as they did during the first half of the twentieth century, progressive practitioners of rhetorical education keep Dewey's practices alive, demonstrated impressively by Stephen M. Fishman and Lucille McCarthy in *John Dewey and the Challenge of Classroom Practice*. The authors have wrestled with the question of student-curriculum ratio and concluded, in the quest for student-curriculum integration, "Teachers must encourage students to find genuine problems which excite their interests, problems which can be explored and ameliorated by engagement with the curriculum" (19).

Hephzibah Roskelly and Kate Ronald also recommend, in *Reason to Believe*, a careful consideration of Dewey and the pragmatist tradition. Amid the social-constructionist, critical-theory, and postmodern emphases in contemporary composition studies, the authors assert that creative, self-consciously contingent teaching still matters in the quest for better life chances for our students and, ultimately, ourselves. They do not see pragmatism's focus on classroom practices to be at odds with theory but construe pragmatism, given its premier concern with outcomes, as germane to the best theorizing. Concerning Cornel West specifically, they consider him a pragmatist extraordinaire, one who exemplifies the notion of "the practice of teaching as the consequence, in action, of the privileged life of the mind and books" (15). Moreover, Roskelly and Ronald are attracted to the connections that West makes between his teaching and his participation in and promotion of various moral and political actions, such actions themselves understood, in pragmatist terms, to be the consequence of West's academic career. The authors make West's project central to their own work by drawing on *The American Evasion of Philosophy* and essays such as "Theory, Pragmatisms, and Politics" and "Beyond Multiculturalism and Eurocentrism." Regarding moral norms, social intervention, resistance, and struggle, they write, "We would like to share West's hope that theory might look again to pragmatism for potential solutions to our culture's ills and that teachers might see the benefits of thinking romantically/pragmatically about the conflicting demands placed on them and their students" (99–100).

But although Roskelly and Ronald clearly possess liberating impulses, and their work is certainly a most admirable political project, they avoid the specific and strident political criticisms made by West with respect to capitalism and empire. The strongest comment they make about systems, referring particularly to educational ones but metaphorically to larger social and political arrangements, is that "it's faculty, who act on their beliefs in the multiple conversations they carry on in and out of the classroom, who can determine whether systems will answer to the human interest or not" (*Reason to Believe* 137). West undoubtedly agrees, though his activist urge makes him desire the acceleration of deliberative processes, and he would exhibit impatience with initiatives like those of Fishman, McCarthy, Roskelly, and Ronald, however stellar, that are linked firmly to pragmatism in the Deweyan grain. These scholars, for instance, make virtually no mention of W. E. B. Du Bois, though Du Bois was crucial to how West conceived the promise of pragmatism.

Whereas West lauded Dewey as the foremost theorist in the tradition of American pragmatism, he celebrated Du Bois as the tradition's most important political activist. Through radical praxis that entailed a social-structural analysis of liberal, capitalist democracy and colonialism, Du Bois, who was a student of James at Harvard University, made pragmatism both African American and international. Du Bois' deep-democratic commitment addressed the struggles of African Americans, the embattled American working class, and the oppressed worldwide.

Early in his career, Du Bois fronted the issue of race as no other pragmatist had or would. Responding to Emerson's notion of double-consciousness, which spoke to the tensions between an American existence and the influence of European culture, Du Bois wrote the oft-quoted passage in *The Souls of Black Folk*:

> The Negro is a sort of seventh son, born with a veil, and gifted with second-sight in this American world—a world which yields him no true self-consciousness, but only lets him see himself through the revelation of the other world. It is a peculiar sensation, this double-consciousness, this sense of always looking at one's self through the eyes of others, of measuring one's soul by the tape of a world that looks on in amused contempt and pity. One ever feels his twoness—an American, a Negro; two souls, two thoughts, two unreconciled strivings, two warring ideals in one dark body, whose dogged strength alone keeps it from being torn asunder. (qtd. in West, *American Evasion* 142)[5]

Whereas Emerson viewed double-consciousness as a condition from which to leap forward into uniquely American expressions of humanity, for Du Bois the dynamic was different (*American Evasion of Philosophy* 142). According to West, "Du Bois' 'double-consciousness' suggested this unique occasion as the *cause* of a problem, a problem resulting precisely from the exercise of white human powers celebrated by Emerson. In short, Du Bois subverts the Emersonian theodicy by situating it within an imperialist and ethnocentric rhetorical and political context" (142–43). In a public career that spanned eight decades and included his involvement in various reformist, civil rights, Pan-Africanist, socialist, antiwar, and anticolonialist initiatives, Du Bois served as a concrete revision of both Emersonian expressionism and Deweyan ethical-democratic vision. By West's account, Du Bois imbued pragmatism with a perspective on the "impetus and impediments to individuality and radical democracy, a perspective that highlights the plight of the wretched of the earth, namely, the majority of humanity who own no property or wealth, participate in no democratic arrangements, and whose individualities are crushed by hard labor and harsh living conditions" (147–48).

Despite the achievements of Dewey, Du Bois, and other American pragmatists such as C. Wright Mills, West recognizes that the tradition as a whole is fraught with problems. He admires the historicism, moral convictions, emphasis on revision, broad social urges, and the desire for communal norms and ameliorative social practices. But he also returns time and again to the philosophical and political weaknesses. For example, an immediate quandary is the question of how one legitimately suggests norms without appeal to a master narrative. If norms and knowledge are grounded in community experience, how wide does the community have to be for the norms and knowledge to be considered valid? As for the issue of foundations, it appears obvious that although the landscape before us can be under perpetual construction, where we stand cannot be under construction, or we cannot stand at all. West addressed this dilemma by arguing in *Prophesy Deliverance!* that pragmatist inquiry involves a "perennial process of dialogue which can question any claim but never all at once" (21). The question still remains of which claims we should tackle first. The pragmatist response, of course, would be to raise the question of what difference does it make how we proceed or how we conceive of or demonstrate knowledge. The main point would be to proceed from where we are, which, in any event, is never nowhere, and then carefully appraise the results that stem from the choices made. But the aim here is not to debate the merits of pragmatism at length. Rather, the goal is to highlight the role the philosophy has played in West's unfolding cultural criticism. Pragmatism can defend itself fairly well, and its ultimate value, particularly for teachers, lies in disturbing, complicating, and challenging otherwise totalizing views of truth, power, and society.

More pressing for West than any philosophical conundrum is that in his mind pragmatism as a whole reflects the Deweyan flaw of not fully accounting for class and has been soft in terms of political action connected not only to class struggle but also in terms of racism and sexism. In *The American Evasion of Philosophy*, he argued that pragmatism, or neopragmatism as he called it at that juncture with specific reference to Rorty, needed to move "beyond its own tradition from Emerson to Rorty—still concerned with human powers, provocation, and personality, [and become] inextricably linked to oppositional analyses of class, race, and gender and oppositional movements for creative democracy and social freedom" (210).

In the end, West described his own form of cultural criticism and political praxis, which he labeled prophetic pragmatism (*American Evasion* 212). Reflecting on the name for his ideas, West commented, "I have dubbed it 'prophetic' in that it harks back to the Jewish and Christian tradition of prophets who brought urgent and compassionate critique to bear on the evils of their day. The mark of the prophet is to speak the truth in love with courage—come what may" (*American Evasion* 233). The defining features of this method are "a universal consciousness that promotes an all-embracing democratic and libertarian moral vision, a historical consciousness that acknowledges human finitude and conditionedness, and a critical consciousness which encourages relentless critique and self-criticism for the aims of social change and personal humility" (*American Evasion* 232). As distilled through everyday experience, prophetic pragmatism makes its viewpoint explicit, speaks to the circumstances of the common folk, and seeks to counter specific and broad instances of racial, gender, and class subjugation along with the attendant social ills. West injected pragmatism with Marxism while withholding total allegiance to either school of thought: "The emancipatory social experimentalism that sits at the center of prophetic pragmatic politics closely resembles the radical democratic elements of Marxist theory, yet its flexibility shuns any dogmatic, a priori, or monistic pronouncements" (*American Evasion* 214).

Mark David Wood, author of *Cornel West and the Politics of Prophetic Pragmatism*, wonders why West holds on to pragmatism so dearly given how severely he qualifies it in order to dissociate pragmatism from cultural conservatism and corporate liberalism, social arrangements that the philosophy, given its flexibility, can be used to justify. Wood, however, is less strident in his critique than were midcentury critics from the organized left, who, if they were around, would give West a rough go of it. Harry K. Wells, for example, wrote a book titled *Pragmatism: Philosophy of Imperialism*, and Harry Selsam, while praising the book, asked, "Is there a possible significance in the fact that the country that developed pragmatism is the country that threatens all mankind with destruction by hydrogen bombs?" ("Marxism vs. Pragmatism," 64). Even a sympathetic Steven Mailloux wonders, "Is neopragmatism an antitheory irrelevant to any specific political program; is it a reactionary defense of traditional institutions; or is it a justification for radical democratic reforms? . . . Does rhetorical pragmatism thus lead to political quietism, because it provides no objective basis for ethical choice; or to social anarchy, because it provides justification for *any* political choice?" (22). In the end, Mailloux maintains that pragmatism does imply a politics, though West would not recognize those vaguely described politics of conversation and potential community as a political program.[6] West's prophetic pragmatism is not reducible to the philosophy of pragmatism that Mailloux discusses. Prophetic pragmatism has a harder edge as a process of continual inquiry, as a discursive strategy for evaluating and reassessing various problems. These include problems of Marxism.

Marxism and the Maze

Composition has enjoyed a fairly long interaction with Marxist theory. Marxism fueled Richard Ohmann's sweeping indictment in *English in America* as he pondered the relationship between English studies and the capitalist state and called for "socialist revolution" (256).[7] Marxism also, in a very specific sense, informed John Trimbur's "Composition and the Circulation of Writing," in which he applied Marx's concepts of circulation, drawn from *Grundrisse*, to forward a more complex notion of writing, one that considers production, distribution, and consumption as well as composing. In short, Trimbur employed Marxism to reconceptualize the canon of delivery as he sought ways to enable wider public participation in civic discourse.

Indeed, nothing sinister exists in classic Marxist thought. As do all great and creative political thinkers, like Thomas Hobbes or Jean-Jacques Rousseau, Marx imaginatively posited a theory of human history that yielded recommended political relationships. He verged close to Rousseau, who said that humans corrupted their basically compassionate nature when they embraced greed. "As soon as they perceived that it was useful for one man to have provisions for two," wrote Rousseau, "equality disappeared, property was introduced, work became necessary, and vast forests were changed into pleasant fields, which had to be watched with human sweat and in which slavery and misery were soon seen to spring up and grow with the crops" (40). So modern social evil resulted from the unequal accumulation of property and not from the passions, as Hobbes decided, that "restless desire of power after power that ceaseth only in death," which was his rationale for social laws (161).[8] For Rousseau, humans had evolved so far from their original state in nature that the best thing to hope for was a decent social contract, the best contract being bourgeois democracy, which was preferable to monarchy or aristocracy even though the laws were primarily a tool of the rich.

Although Marx also speculated about human nature, he viewed history in terms of successive stages of economic organization, feudalism giving way to capitalism, for example, and as a series of class struggles, one's class being determined, as well as one's consciousness, by one's position relative to the means of production. A key point is that workers create surplus value, in other words, generate far more wealth than the salaries they are paid. Enormous amounts, just plain mad loot, go into the pockets of those who control land, technology, and capital. Any ideas the bourgeoisie put forward to justify capitalist relations is mere *ideology*, and any other thinking that fails to account for capitalist relations in terms of class antagonism is *false consciousness*. The upshot is that workers in alliance with the members of the middle class who identify their interests with those of the workers will overthrow (wouldn't be history's first revolution) the bourgeoisie and eventually exert democratic control over the means of production in a society in which the state apparatus withers away almost as casually as a setting sun.[9] Marx never detailed how this imagined society would function, yet Marxism conjures up visions in the mass American imaginary of lunatic radicals and totalitarian governments. It is situated somewhere close to dim recall of George Orwell's *Animal Farm*.

Cornel West, though not a Marxist, has long considered Marxism to be a valuable approach, pointing in *Prophesy Deliverance!* to its democratic thrust and then enlarging that assessment in a second book, *The Ethical Dimensions of Marxist Thought*. West thinks that workers exerting control over the modes of production is fundamentally democratic, and he correctly believes that Marx is a product of European Romanticism that reached its high point with the French Revolution. In a 1992 interview with Eva Corredor, he stated, "Once you link the values of flourishing individuality, a profoundly Romantic notion, with the expansion of democratic operations and practices, I argue that you are at the ethical core of the Marxist project" (60). In the same interview, West referred to Marx's understanding of the "interlocking relation between corporate, financial and political elites who had access to a disproportionate amount of resources, power, prestige and status in society" (59). West saw this as a crucial starting point for understanding the political system of the United States. He figured that if we lose sight of this relationship, "we have little or no analytic tools in our freedom fight" (59). In the introduction to *The Ethical Dimensions of Marxist Thought*, he remarked, concerning Marx bashing, "It is often assumed that vulgar Marxist thought exhausts the Marxist tradition—as if monocausal accounts of history, essentialist conceptions of society or reductionist readings of culture are all Marxist thought has to offer. One wonders whether any such critics have read Marx's *Eighteenth Brumaire*, *Class Struggles in France* or the *Grundrisse*" (xxiii). We know that Trimbur has.

A problem West sees is that Marxism has been so distorted by practitioners over the past 150 years that one can feel trapped in a maze trying to find its progressive praxis. In *Prophesy Deliverance!*

he identified six major "streams" in the Marxist tradition, only one of which he recognized as progressive.[10] He characterized the Leninist stream, with its vanguard party and central committee, as right wing. Even more so are the Stalinist stream and its dictatorial enactment. Trotskyism is not considered as bad as Stalinism, but its essentially Leninist makeup also makes it a right-wing movement in West's estimation. He sees all three of those streams to be polluted by authoritarianism, dogma, and elitism.

Another stream is Gramscian, after Italian Marxist Antonio Gramsci, whom West acknowledged, echoing the opinion of editors Quintin Hoare and Geoffrey Smith, as the "most penetrating Marxist theorist of culture in this [twentieth] century" (*Prophesy Deliverance!* 118). Gramsci extended Marxist thought by providing an elaborate account of cultural and discursive elements, such as, race, patriarchy, and religion, that are not bound in a determinate fashion to an economic base but that nonetheless play a major role in dominance and the maintenance of the status quo. Although dissent is necessarily present, the net effect of a society's discursive practices, a crucial observation in Gramsci's rubric, is that the populace actively consents to the rule of the dominant social class. Marx and Frederick Engels wrote in *The German Ideology* and later in *The Communist Manifesto*, "The ruling ideas of each age have ever been the ideas of its ruling class" (59).[11] So Marxism from the beginning expressed succinctly a concern with discourse. But Gramsci explored more the cultural contours attached to the claim and saw the battle over discourse and political dominance as open ended. No particular class is guaranteed dominance in perpetuity.

Gramsci's ideas have had a major impact on progressive scholars in composition because schooling is an aspect of civil society tied directly to the issue of hegemony.[12] When compositionists speak of dominant discourses and counterhegemonic linguistic practices, when they express interest in the questions of "traditional intellectuals," "organic intellectuals," "new intellectuals," and "permanent persuaders," they are echoing Gramscian sentiments.[13] Victor Villanueva Jr. makes extensive use of Gramscian analysis in his memoir *Bootstraps: From an American Academic of Color* (122–38). Romy Clark and Roz Ivanič provide a clear exposition of the relationship between Gramscian thought and the power dynamics of writing in *The Politics of Writing* (20–36). Although drawn to the work of Gramsci, West ultimately judged the Gramscian stream to occupy a center-right position because he was suspicious of Gramsci's "neo-Leninism" (*Prophesy Deliverance!* 137).

A fifth stream flows from the work of Eduard Bernstein, a strident anticommunist who believed that "evolutionary socialism" could be achieved through legislative maneuvering and electoral politics. Bernstein's position is enlightened within the tradition of Marxism, according to West, but overall he feels that Bernsteinism is too comfortable with the capitalist order.

West lauded "councilism," a form of left-wing Marxism derived from the work of Anton Pannekoek, Karl Korsch, the martyred Rosa Luxemburg, and others as *the* progressive stream. Councilism emphasizes local councils, hence its name, rather than vanguard parties, central committees, or repressive bureaucracies. And it fails to cozy up to liberal capitalism. West summarized, "Councilism is committed first and foremost to the norms of individuality and democracy within the workers (and other progressive) movements—and within the future socialist society" (*Prophesy Deliverance!* 137).

While West can determine a progressive Marxism that represents a humane response to economic exploitation and class oppression, he still views Marxist theory as insufficient. He confided to Corredor in an interview, "Marxism simply does not speak to the levels of psycho-cultural politics. You need Freud . . . and you need novels, you need the blues and spirituals, a whole host of other insights (64). In "Race and Social Theory," he issued a more expansive and explicit critique.

> My basic disagreement with Marxist theory is twofold. First, I hold that many social practices, such as racism, are best understood and explained not only or primarily by locating them within modes of production, but also by situating them within the cultural traditions of civilizations. This permits me to highlight the specificity of those practices that traverse or cut across different modes of production, for example, racism, religion, patriarchy, homophobia. Focusing on racist practices or white-supremacist logics operative in premodern, modern and postmodern Western civilization yields both racial continuity and discontinuity. Even Marxist theory can be shown to be both critical and captive to a Eurocentrism that can justify racist practices. And though Marxist theory remains indispensable, it also obscures and hides the ways in which secular ideologies—especially modern ideologies of scientism, racism and

sexual hedonism (Marxist theory does better with nationalism, professionalism and consumerism)—are linked to larger civilizational ways of life and struggle. (267)

In short, neither the hard economism of Marx nor the sharp cultural insights of Gramsci suffice for West as a theory of culture applicable to the modern state. West's second objection expressed on that occasion concerned the solipsism of Marxism and its ties to a European will to truth and power.

> I claim that the Marxist obsession with the economic sphere as the major explanatory factor is itself a reflection of the emergence of Marxist discourse in the midst of an industrial capitalism preoccupied with economic production; and, more important, this Marxist obsession is itself a symptom of a particular Western version of the will to truth and style of rationality that valorizes control, mastery and domination of nature and history. I neither fully reject this will to truth, nor downplay the crucial role of the economic sphere in social and historical explanation. But one is constrained to acknowledge the methodological point about the degree to which Marxist theory remains inscribed within the very problematic of the unfreedom and domination it attempts to overcome. (267–68)

The diminished use by West of Marxist analysis troubles observers like Wood, who sort of wonders whether West hasn't become a Bernsteinian himself, intellectually accepting of capitalism. Neither Marxism nor pragmatism, for that matter, is mentioned in *Democracy Matters*, though West has not abandoned class as an analytic category. He states clearly that the struggle is against imperialism. What is modern Western imperialism but capitalism searching the globe?

Whatever one feels about the status of West's current affinities for Marxism, it should be understood that a critique of Marxism appeared in his corpus at the outset. He always declared himself a Marxist-influenced but non-Marxist social critic. In any case, the vision of Marx or Luxemburg was never going to be the primary prophecy in West's thinking. A Christianity that could not be dislodged got there first.

Prophetic Christianity as Foundation

Prophetic Christianity mightily informs West's interest in the free individual belonging to a freedom-loving social group. Despite the checkered history of Christian institutions, he believes, "The basic contribution of prophetic Christianity . . . is that every individual regardless of class, country, caste, race, or sex should have the opportunity to fulfill his or her potentialities. This first and fundamental norm is the core of the prophetic Christian gospel" (*Prophesy Deliverance!* 16). The tenets of secular progressivism are thus fused with Christian prophetic witness, thereby synthesizing the best of the Marxist and Christian viewpoints. In *Prophesy Deliverance!* West argued that the two systems of thought are united in their "commitment to the negation of what is and the transformation of prevailing realities in light of the norms of individuality and democracy" (101). As is the case with Marxism, contradictions lie at the heart of the Christian gospel. But these contradictions are not seen to stem from an economic base and its ramifications in a superstructure. The conflict in Christianity is between the fallen *nature* of humans and the desire to do good. Dignified and socially concerned people collide with the depraved and indifferent. Often times the dignity-depravity dialectic takes place *within* persons. In either case, the will to social amelioration is ceaselessly at odds with resistance and refusal (17).

Furthermore, West explained in *Prophesy Deliverance!* that prophetic Christianity embodies two interlocking notions of freedom, existential freedom, which is the "divine gift of grace," and social freedom, which provides a rationale for progressive social activism and the quest for democracy (18). Nonetheless, the prophetic Christian project, even that informed by Marxism, is labeled "impotent" by West in the sense that it cannot conceptualize the transcendence of humankind's blemishes and project victory within the process of human history (96). As he expounded, "Ultimate triumph indeed depends on the almighty power of a transcendent God who proleptically acts in history but who also withholds the final, promised negation and transformation of history until an unknown future" (96). Yet the transformative effort must go on because conceptual impotence should not preclude action given that substantial betterment, though not perfection, is attainable (96). In *Prophesy Deliverance!* therefore, we see the fusion of philosophical, political, cultural, and religious perspectives that reflected, in West's words, "an Afro-American Revolutionary Christianity."[14]

Almost immediately after the appearance of *Prophesy Deliverance!* West began to extend and refine his notions, particularly in regard to the ethics of social struggle, along with beginning to range in his concern with prophetic Christianity, as has been the case with his engagement with American pragmatism, beyond a specifically African American critical method. He tirelessly tried to wrest rhetorical control from the Religious Right, asserting in a 1984 essay titled "Religion, Politics, Language," "The Moral Majority employs the divisive language of 'Christians vs. Others' (e.g., modernists, pagans, homosexuals, etc.), whereas prophetic black Christians used the language of rights and common good" (24). The same year, in a piece titled "The Prophetic Tradition in Afro-America," he wrote, "The distinctive features of prophetic activity are Pascalian leaps of faith in the capacity of human beings to transform their circumstances, engage in relentless criticism and self-criticism, and project visions, analyses, and practices of social freedom" (38). In 1986, at a symposium on Martin Luther King Jr., whom West considers to be the "most significant and successful organic intellectual in American history," he asserted, "Fundamentalist Christianity is *rationalistic* in orientation and *legalistic* in effect, hence it leans toward bibliolatry; whereas black evangelical Christianity is *dramatic* in orientation and *moralistic* in effect, hence it affirms a biblically informed perspective" ("Martin Luther King Jr." 7; emphasis in the original). But he later sharpened the definition of moralistic, making a distinction between moralistic acts and moral actions. In "The Crisis in Contemporary American Religion," he noted that moralistic acts perform restricted and even restrictive service because they are expressly rooted in sentimentalism, not in more far-reaching social concern. In other words, "Moralistic acts rest upon a narrow, parochial anti-intellectualism that sees only pitiful individuals, whereas moral action is based on a broad, robust prophetism that highlights systemic social analysis of the circumstances under which tragic persons struggle" (x).

In *Democracy Matters*, West remarks simply that prophetic witness is predicated upon the divine love of justice and notes that prophets like Amos, Jeremiah, and Isaiah were not interested solely in individual conversion but in mass ameliorative action. He quotes from Proverbs 14:31, "He who oppresses a poor man insults his maker; he who is kind to the needy honors him" (17). In contemporary terms, the thinking follows, prophetic witness should target authoritarianism, aggressive militarism, and irresponsible wealth. To West, the best of the Judeo-Christian and Islamic traditions "should inform and embolden the struggle against the callous indifference of the plutocratic elites of the American empire about the sufferings of our own poor and oppressed peoples. It should also help to illuminate the effects of our imperialism on the poor and oppressed peoples around the world" (19).

Rosemary Cowan, writing in *Cornel West: The Politics of Redemption*, contends that West's oeuvre is best understood in the context of liberation theology, although West has refused the label of theologian because he would not presume to possess a sufficient understanding of God. Yet, Cowan argues that West's rejection devalues his work because liberation theology is its unifying element, resolves any seeming inconsistencies, and renders it fully coherent (15). She identifies him as a liberation theologian on at least six counts: (1) his democratic and nondogmatic approach that questions society and church hierarchies, (2) his criticism of inadequate forms of democracy and Christianity, (3) his view of God as siding with the oppressed and his privileging of emancipatory action over any particular line of political science or social theory, (4) his understanding of history as open ended and his belief in the possibilities of human agency, (5) his historicizing of spirituality in relation to specific contexts and problems, and (6) his embrace of Christianity as existentially empowering while he simultaneously accepts aspects of Marxism (12–13).

Cowan's case seems reasonable despite the fact that she restricts the scope of West's concerns to the plight of African Americans, which is a mistake no researcher should have made as late as 2003. Nonetheless, she writes rather persuasively.

> Political theology embraces systems of thought such as communitarianism and socialism, and the concerns of political theology and political theory coalesce in areas such as justice, power, freedom, utopia, and democracy. Thinking specifically of West, the political themes of justice, identity and difference, coalition building, democracy, socialism, and the common good are all important for his liberation theology. He also generalizes about human capacities, attempts to define the nature of their shared obligations, and offers a critique of prevailing forms of unjust power. While his basis for this is Christian rather than secular principles, his work attempts to fulfill the same function as other political theories. (17)

Of course, there is no way to tease out legitimately any subbasis for reaction. One responds out of everything that one is, knows, and believes, not in a compartmentalized fashion. It suffices to claim that Christianity is a crucial foundation for him.

Christianity also is, though not necessarily the prophetic type, important to many of our students. James Moffett was aware of the secular bent of a significant number of professors: "I know, the university feels it shouldn't play doctor or priest, dirty its hands with therapy and its mind with religion. But if it has real live students on its hands, its hands are already dirty" (Interchanges 261). Moffett argued further that intellectuals need to "quit confusing spirituality with superstition and sectarianism," and he noted, "unhealed wounds and undeveloped souls will thwart the smartest curriculum" (261). West would support Moffett's argument in the hope but not necessarily the expectation that such attention to spirituality and religion would lead students in the direction of democracy and humanism.

African American Humanism and Tragicomic Hope

In the eyes of Cornel West, one must take culture seriously in any effort to develop effective praxis. In this regard, he draws heavily, though not exclusively, on what he described in *Prophesy Deliverance!* as the African American humanist tradition, artistic production that promotes the vitality and vigor of African American life and is an exemplar of the tragicomic hope that he describes in more detail in later works. As with other strands of inquiry, West branched out from a specific concern with African American life and talked more broadly about humanism and the tragicomic. But because products of African American culture are the basis for the discussion of tragicomic hope in chapter 5, I focus this particular commentary about humanism and the tragicomic on African American experience.

In *Prophesy Deliverance!* West outlined four traditions of African American response to the group's sojourn in America (69–91). There is exceptionalism, or a belief in African American uniqueness, an idea he associated with the early work of W. E. B. Du Bois, most of the writers of the Harlem Renaissance and the Black Arts Movement, Elijah Muhammad, the early Malcolm X, and Martin Luther King Jr., among others. There is assimilationism, or the view that African American culture is pathological, a position attributed mainly to E. Franklin Frazier; marginalism, or the individualism and alienation he sensed in figures like Sutton Griggs, Charles Chesnutt, Nella Larsen, Richard Wright, and James Baldwin. And there is humanism, or the superior achievement, which he felt was reflected in the words of Langston Hughes, Zora Neale Hurston, Sterling Brown, Paul Robeson, the later Du Bois, and the later Malcolm X. To West, African

American humanism makes no ontological assertions of inferiority or superiority, treats African Americans as humans like everyone else, and assumes the universal content of African American expressive forms. West developed the idea.

> The humanist self-image of Afro-Americans is one neither of heroic superhumans untouched by the experience of oppression nor pathetic subhumans devoid of a supportive culture. This tradition does not romanticize or reject Afro-American culture; instead, it accepts this culture for what it is, "the expression of an oppressed human community imposing its distinctive form of order on an existential chaos, explaining its political predicament, preserving its self-respect, and projecting its own special hopes for the future" (85).

Moreover, African American humanism promotes individuality and democratic processes and shuns the "self-serving pursuit of status, wealth, and prestige" (90–91).

For West, the best examples of African American humanism are the spirituals, the blues, gospel, and jazz: "Afro-American musicians are Afro-American humanists *par excellence*" (*Prophesy Deliverance!* 86). Ralph Ellison held the same rank for him among African American literary artists (*Prophesy Deliverance!* 89). By this point, however, West's taxonomy shows signs of strain. One problem is his characterization of King as a weak variety of exceptionalist, one who "seemed to believe that Afro-Americans possess a unique proclivity for nonviolence, more so than do other racial groups, that they have a certain bent toward humility, meekness, and forbearance, hence are quite naturally disposed toward nonviolent action" (*Prophesy Deliverance!* 75). The King who once kept guns to guard his home, during a time when Wyatt T. Walker and others who marched with him were armed, the King who was begged to disarm by Bayard Rustin, the King who labored so hard to exhort somewhat impatient followers to remain civilly disobedient and witnessed the inception of the Black Power Movement, certainly harbored no illusions that black people were uniquely disposed toward nonviolence.[15] King continually pleaded for folks to put away their weapons. If he thought African Americans were naturally so meek, he would not have worked so hard to keep them peaceful. In addition, it is strange that King, the great organic intellectual, as West said, whose humanism prompted him to speak out against the imperialist war in Vietnam, occupies a lower rung than Ellison, the "humanist *par excellence*," who supported the war and criticized King for speaking out.[16] It could also be argued that while the collective humanist achievement of black musicians can hardly be denied, the mere fact that an African American plays music does not make him or her a humanist in the political sense that West meant. And a simple assertion that Robeson was more humanist than Wright or suffered less alienation is far from convincing.[17] But although some of West's specific takes on African American cultural figures left something to be desired, his expression of an African American humanist ideal was powerful overall and, in any event, still represents an important part of his overall message.

West's notion of African American humanism is linked, as is all of his work, to a conception of the tragic. He argued in *The American Evasion of Philosophy*, "The brutalities and atrocities in human history, the genocidal attempts in this century and the present-day barbarities require that those who accept the progressive and prophetic designations put forth some sense of the tragic" (227). He felt that such articulation "tempers utopian impulse with a profound sense of the tragic character of life and history" (228). Part of his case for prophetic pragmatism relied on the fact that it unflinchingly examined personal and institutional evil while not expecting to eliminate it all. Some of this may seem like intellectual piling on by West and cause for a whistle and a penalty. After all, an understanding of tragedy and evil is implied in prophetic Christianity. To belabor the point appears to be more a chance to acknowledge the influence of Raymond Williams's *Modern Tragedy* than anything else. More to the point, or at least my point, is that West tied African American humanism and the tragic to the comic and offered this blend as an essential description of black cultural output and life. In "Subversive Joy and Revolutionary Patience in Black Christianity," he wrote:

> The radically comic character of Afro-American life—the pervasive sense of play, laughter and ingenious humor of blacks—flows primarily from the profound Afro-American Christian preoccupation with the tragedy in the struggle for freedom and the freedom in a tragic predicament. This comic release is the black groan made gay. Yet this release is neither escapist nor quietistic. Rather, it is *engaged gaiety*, *subversive joy* and *revolutionary patience*, which works for and looks to the kingdom to come. . . . It is tragic in that it tempers exorbitant expectations. This perspective precludes political disillusionment and its product, misanthropic nihilism." (165)

This is the "sad yet sweet indictment" and the "melancholic yet ame-lioristic stance" that West speaks of in *Democracy Matters* and that infuses much of African American music (216). Even African American music not strictly of this character is closely related to such a blues sensibility. Composition has made ample use of black music—Elaine Richardson, Gwendolyn Pough, and Adam Banks immediately come to mind—as crucial rhetorical artifacts of black existence.[18]

Sprouting New Branches

In the preface to the twentieth-anniversary edition of *Prophesy Deliverance!* West reaffirmed his embrace of American pragmatism—and American jazz—asserting that such embrace reflects his devotion to "polyphonic inquiry and improvisational conversation" (8). These ideas also resonate, though with less-explicit Marxism and renewed attention to prophetic Christianity and the tragicomic, in *Democracy Matters*. But the regulating categories are different: Socratic commitment, prophetic witness, and tragicomic hope. Socratic commitment is a reconfiguring of pragmatism. Prophetic witness is an amalgam of prophetic Christianity—and Islam—and the insights of progressive Marxism along with apprehension of the tragic. Tragicomic hope, West's fondness for Anton Chekhov aside, stems from prophetic Christianity and African American humanism, especially the lessons of African American music.

3
Socratic Commitment and Critical Literacy

CONNECTED TO Deweyan speculations about critical intelligence, "critical literacy" took hold as a term in composition studies during the 1970s as the work of Paulo Freire gained ascendance and was engaged by scholars like Ann Berthoff, Henry Giroux, Donaldo Macedo, and Ira Shor.[1] In *Pedagogy of the Oppressed*, Freire writes the seemingly oxymoronic phrase, "freedom is acquired by conquest" (31). However, he did not mean by conquest the subjugation of others. He meant that people had to work for freedom by recognizing the causes of their oppression, a recognition that is necessary to the task of social transformation. This heightened perception, or *conscientizacao*, is to be used to identify the specific social, economic, and political contradictions to be transcended. Freire understood that language is a crucial aspect of liberation because only through "naming the world," imprinting one's own discursive construal on the environment, can one have a chance to participate in it on one's own terms. Education is deemed authentic, therefore, to the extent that it demands active student involvement and deliberately aids in the formation of student critical consciousness. "Authentic education," Freire states classically, "is not carried on by 'A' for 'B' or by 'A' about 'B,' but rather by 'A' with 'B,' mediated by the world—a world which challenges both parties giving rise to views or opinions about it" (82). Literacy, in this view, is critical social practice, not the mere acquisition or transmission of technical skills. Or as Giroux elaborates in the introduction to Freire and Macedo's volume *Literacy: Reading the Word and the World*, "Literacy is best understood as a myriad of discursive forms and cultural competencies that construct and make available the various relations and experiences that exist between learners and the world" (10). Critical literacy is, he continues, "both a narrative for agency as well as a referent for critique" (10). In an essay titled "What Is Literacy?" Shor adds, "Critical literacy can be thought of as a social practice itself and as a tool for the study of other social practices" (10). When I think of the difference between functional literacy and critical literacy, I often recall little Pecola Breedlove of Toni Morrison's splendid first novel *The Bluest Eye*. Pecola could decode the primer containing the dominant and *dominating* white, suburban, Dick-and-Jane narrative, but to her demise, she could neither deconstruct that story nor resist it.

Cornel West considers Freire to have been an exemplary intellectual and practitioner. In "Paulo Freire," he lauded the educator's project of "democratic dialogue" that was "attuned to the concrete operations of power (in and out of the classroom)" (179). He feels that Freirean-style, Socratic questioning is much needed today as we grapple with public discourse, particularly as such discourse is influenced by the media. Decrying that market values drive many media decisions, he contends that corporate media are largely responsible for constricting and constraining political dialogue, which he describes as "so formulaic, so tailored into poll-driven, focus-group-approved slogans that don't really say anything substantive or strike at the core of our lived experience" (*Democracy Matters* 64). Moreover, he is critical of entertainment broadcasts masquerading as insightful news, a turn of events that represents the dominance of titillation over useful testimony. The desired role of the media as a fair, balanced, and fundamental component of a critical democracy has been compromised, in West's view, by what he terms "vulgar partisanship" (*Democracy Matters* 38).

The Practice of Critical Literacy

For composition instructors, who teach many media consumers, there is hope in the general study of Freire and West and in specific rhetorical schema like those of Donald Lazere, who makes critical thinking about politics central to his classroom. Responding deftly to claims by the likes of Maxine Hairston that composition courses should not be politicized, Lazere knows that they already have been overly politicized, ensconced rather tamely within a white supremacist, patriarchal, capitalist norm. Ironically, he depoliticizes the classroom or at least disrupts hegemonic comfort by establishing politics as the main and express object of rhetorical inquiry. He enables students to consider a wide array of ideological perspectives and develop facility in interrogating those positions, the very activities that should lie at the heart of civic literacy and humanistic education. Although he himself leans toward democratic socialism, Lazere would not favor any attempt to impose upon students any particular political analysis. He believes that through his method, "the left agenda of prompting students to question the subjectivity underlying socially constructed modes of thinking can be reconciled with the conservative agenda of objectivity and nonpartisanship" (260). An eyebrow or two should be raised at the suggestion that the conservative agenda is as benign as Lazere characterizes it to be. Nonetheless, his pedagogical project is on point. He teaches units like "Political Semantics," "Psychological Blocks to Perceiving Bias," "Modes of Biased and Deceptive Rhetoric," and "Locating and Evaluating Partisan Sources." In addition, he distributes appendixes that contain definitions and taxonomies. On the sheet titled "American Media and Commentators from Left to Right," listed between Roger Wilkins and Michael Lerner is the name Cornel West (270). West, of course, would affirm Lazere's pursuit of the "Emersonian mission of bringing to bear on current events the longer view, the synthesizing vision needed to counteract the hurriedness, atomization, and ideological hodgepodge that debase our public discourse as well as our overdepartmentalized curricula and overspecialized scholarship" (261).

My students and I have been wrestling, mostly honestly, with these issues. Not surprisingly, many of these students have begun class by echoing sentiments about liberal media bias. Their first resistant move, such as it is, is usually against what they perceive as liberal, leftist, pluralist pedagogy. Like Lazere, it is not their politics that I am invested in changing but their rhetorical and hermeneutical abilities (though I never claim to be completely even-handed and never mind if their politics do drift leftward). Most important is that they begin to understand discourse as constitutive, though not all-determinative, and commit to making up their own minds insofar as possible. I pointed out to the thirty-four students in my undergraduate "Rhetorical Traditions" course that it would be hard for them to participate meaningfully in a discussion about socialism, a term we encountered while reading liberal linguist Robin Lakoff's *Language War*, when not one of them could offer a definition of the term (true story). Lakoff, however, understands my students' predicament as she explains that *socialism* in the mainstream American vocabulary is a word that operates devoid of any real semantic weight, that is, any connection to ideas about a system of economics. The word only functions pragmatically as an insult (67). This is so, Lakoff asserts, for at least a couple of reasons. Drawing upon the idea of "frames," particularly as developed by scholars like Stephen Levinson and Deborah Tannen, Lakoff explains that frames are a part of our cognitive apparatus and accumulated knowledge that structure our expectations and determine what we consider normal or unmarked (47). Not every frame results from the imposition of a dominant discourse—the frame by which I carefully avoid fire is an example—but the general concept of frames is closely related to the Gramscian idea of hegemony. Even more closely related is Roland Barthes's idea of *exnomination* that Lakoff borrows, that is, the notion that the ruling class hides behind language in the sense that their viewpoints become normalized and passed on as self-evident or natural. The bourgeoisie, in Barthes's mind, is "*the social class which does not want to be named*" (qtd. in *The Language War* 53–54; emphasis in the original).[2] Therefore, in American culture, capitalism occupies the invisible, unmarked, dominant, commonsense, exnominated rhetorical position. Overall, Lakoff notes the discursive power of norms, "Conservative argumentation strikes many critics as somehow 'smarter' than the ideas of the opposite side. They are smart precisely because they are conservative, tested by time, and neutral" (56).

To illustrate Lakoff's point, I gave the students in that course and in another undergraduate course titled "Contemporary Theories of Reading and Writing" one of my "favorite" language items from the Rupert Murdoch–owned *New York Post*. On July 13, 2001, the paper published on its front page an e-mail by Sunny Liang, a New York City high school history teacher, written to an editor at the newspaper. The e-mail was topped by the paper's headline that proclaimed, "READ THIS E-MAIL." Below the e-mail was the revelation about the occupation of its author. The earth-shattering, totally newsworthy, front-page e-mail:

Only if our society realize that there are so many factors contributing to a student's test score, then the teachers will be willing to take the blam game. Who is to blam when students don't do homeworks? Who is to blam when pareants don't care to come to the pareant conference? Who is to blam when so many of our students come to school without note books and pencils? The problem is we have too many of these students in our society. If you give me an Ap's or honor's class, I do anything the city, the society, or the nation asks me to do. But if you give me these studnets who are failing right from the beginning, I don't want to be responsible for their failure.

Concerning Mr. Liang's gripes about his job, we may disagree with his analysis at some level or think that perhaps he should complicate his discussion of responsibility to include consideration of, say, ethnicity, class, and method. Notwithstanding, he has shared a view that could initiate a serious conversation about teaching in urban settings. And his basic premise is not a hard one with which to sympathize. Liang essentially stated that if people wanted him to take the weight for poor student performance, then they should at least set him up in the most favorable work environment. That could hardly be a more reasonable request. Yet, the reporters who covered the story termed Liang's argument incoherent, ridiculed him, and argued that he was symptomatic of what was wrong with the school system. They quoted the board of education president offering the opinion that she was embarrassed by the letter, which she said indicated that teaching quality was worse than she might have thought. An accompanying article in the same issue featured students expressing similar embarrassment. An article in the following day's issue of the paper featured the chancellor of the New York City system complaining about incompetent teachers in the system.

But a careful examination of Liang's letter reveals other realities. Far from not making sense, it contains a clear line of argument, uses interrogatives with effectiveness, and even features three complex sentences that are each punctuated in accord with standard rules of usage. He misspells a couple of words and has an agreement problem or two, but his point is made quite directly. The editor knew exactly what Liang had argued and even took the opportunity to agree with him that "punk kids," a phrase Liang did *not* use, were the most significant problem in New York City schools. The reporters, who also really knew what Liang argued, focused on his "grammatical errors," a phrase the caption writer used and a term that is an oxymoron. Strictly speaking, in the language of linguists, *grammatical* means correct. If an utterance is wrong relative to the rules of a given language variety, it is ungrammatical. It is not a "grammatical" error. (When I made this point in a textbook manuscript I was helping to prepare, an anonymous reviewer thought I was needlessly quibbling over semantics.) At any rate, sympathetic or neutral readers understood what the caption writer meant because they knew how "grammatical error," imprecise as it is, often is deployed. Generously, they focused on the argument made by the paper, though the paper would not focus on the argument made by Liang.

If we push the analysis further, we can see that the reporters do not take up seriously the question of Liang's qualifications to teach history. There is no discussion of what he actually can do in a classroom or of the conditions under which he labors. The space they use (and the publisher and editor give them) is not to have an informed discussion about the issues raised by Liang but to push a dominant ideological position about language. In short, if it ain't Standardized English, even in your e-mails, you must be incompetent and most likely stupid. Although generally not a betting man, I would lay long odds that the reporters could not write in a Chinese language anywhere near as competently as Liang did in English.

My students grasped the points that I made concerning the piece about Liang, though they had points of their own to make, and some even sided with the reporters in the final analysis. Conservative language ideology, with its often-accompanying racist overtones, undertones, and directly-in-the-middle tones cannot be dispelled so easily, as Lakoff knows. But the key point for me was that none of my students thought the reporters were neutral, objectively reporting the "news." I encouraged them to draw their own conclusions to whatever extent that can be accomplished inside constitutive discourses.

As our conversation about language ideology and media coverage unfolded, I shared with my students an experience I had with an editor of another conservative newspaper, the *Washington Times*. As the Ebonics controversy crested early in 1997, an editor from the *Times* reached me at Syracuse University, where I was on the faculty, to ask if I would write the "pro" position on Ebonics for the point-counterpoint column that the newspaper featured in its weekly magazine insert *Insight on the News*. However, he made it evident that he considered me more or less foil for the "con" side.[3] He wondered what I would write and opined, "All of your leaders think it's a bad idea." He then informed me that the onus would be on me to prove that Ebonics-based educational initiatives actually work. To him, that was the only legitimate path before me.

I took the space, the check, and wrote exactly what I desired. For one, I never specified who *my* leaders were. Neither did I take it upon myself to demonstrate empirically that any particular education program worked. I think that any method of reading or writing ever devised can be shown by some study and from some perspective to work for someone at some time. It all depends on the methodology, the definition of *works*, and a willingness to turn a blind eye to failure. The more germane question for me is whether an educational proposal presents a reasonable response to a clearly identified problem. The African American students in the Oakland, California, school district carried a cumulative 1.8 average, compared to the system-wide average of 2.4 and a 2.7 mark for white students. Although black students were 53 percent of the district population, they represented 80 percent of the suspensions and 71 percent of the student population designated "special needs." At the same time, black students at the Prescott Elementary School, the only school in the district that made instructional use of Ebonics, were performing above average (Perry and Delpit xi). Surely, a reasonable discussion of Ebonics was to be had. In any case, that teachers understand and respond supportively to the language of their students' nurture, given how important language is to identity and given the academic penalties that African American students have historically paid because of exclusionary language practices, is, while not a guarantee of success, a rational response. Rather than use the column to attempt to prove empirically the efficacy of any curriculum project, I used the space to contextualize the Ebonics question and try to bring the light of linguistic theory to heated debates about slang, dialect, and the legitimacy of referring to Ebonics as a language. I also indicated that legal precedent, as well as the educational theories of people like Basil Bernstein, was on the side of the Oakland school board. Not all of my students bought into my arguments, but they all knew that the *Washington Times*, even while publishing both pro and con sides, was far from impartial about Ebonics. One last piece of information I shared about my involvement in the Ebonics controversy, to undermine the idea that the media are biased toward liberals, is that I received a second phone call, this time from a newspaper reporter in Connecticut. She said she had basically finished her article about the damage of Ebonics and was searching for a language expert to validate her viewpoint. Thus she had been referred to me. You can imagine the brevity of that conversation. Not quite as short as two words but not much longer.

Newly Critical but Not New Criticism

No matter how carefully a teacher approaches politics, things can turn dicey. My Bill O'Reilly fans, sensing my own leanings, kick up a pretty good fuss, though I have fared better in recent classes than communications scholar Robert McChesney. I do not mind contentiousness, and I do not push for consensus. However, to establish that civility is to be our tone and that we will value inquiry over dogma, I often start my courses by having students read Shirley Jackson's "A Fine Old Firm." At first, my students barely tolerate this story. In a small-town setting, Mrs. Friedman drops in on Mrs. Concord and her daughter Helen at the suggestion of her son, Bob Friedman, who is stationed overseas in the army with Charlie, Mrs. Concord's son. Charlie has even corresponded with Mrs. Friedman, thanking her for tobacco she sent him. After the Concord women welcome her to their home, they exchange pleasantries and commentary, which mostly focuses on the two sons, though it is also apparent that Mrs. Friedman knows much more about the Concords than they know about her. As she prepares to leave, Mrs. Friedman explains that her husband may be interested in Charlie, whose law studies had been interrupted by military service, joining his firm some day. At this point, Mrs. Concord politely informs Mrs. Friedman that her son is destined to join the firm of Satterthwaite & Harris—"a fine old firm"—of which his great-grandfather used to be a partner. The encounter ends with a chorus of friendly goodbyes. Because the story is brief (barely twelve hundred words) and the language is relatively simple, the reader's quest for meaning can be specified rather easily as part of class discussion. Furthermore, the subject matter has proven to be familiar yet removed enough not to be threatening. As part of this exercise, I usually have students form groups and compose collective responses. As West opined, "The populace deliberating is creative democracy in the making" (*American Evasion of Philosophy* 213).

One group asserted flatly, "There is no point to the story." A second conceded that the story might have a point but that they were unable to find it. They didn't care about the characters or the conversation, instead feeling, "like we were a child who has been dragged from the house with our mother on some errand when she runs into an acquaintance and has to chit-chat, while we impatiently wait for her to shut up so we can leave." Several other groups responded to a perceived social tension in the text, though they did not elaborate (and I had not asked or expected them to do a lot in that regard). Some students thought the story, which contains, in their words, "a great deal of 'build-up' situations with no real conflict or resolution," was a chapter excerpted from a much longer work. They were confident they would discern the "greater meaning" if they had the chance to read the entire book. One group of students was a bit more adventurous (or more conforming to teacher expectation), suggesting, "Everything has a deeper meaning—the clothes, what the women are doing, and the parcels being sent to the boys." In terms of determining conflict, these students argued, "Mrs. Friedman obviously comes from a higher class. This story shows such social inequity between the two families. In the end, Mrs. Concord rejects the charity of Mrs. Friedman in an effort to keep her dignity."

Of the responses I received, the only one I did not affirm was the hypothesis about pointlessness. Why, I asked, would an acclaimed writer (I withhold Jackson's name until later) write a story with no point, if that were possible? And why would someone publish it? And why would your pretty reasonable professor, a guy definitely with points, give it to you to read? The students quickly allowed that the tale cannot be totally devoid of meaning; "no point" was more a statement of impatience and, I would add, rigidity. From there, the class discussed the characteristics of a good critical read. Students had all embraced the common notion that you can write anything about the text you want as long as you use evidence to back it up. What they had thought less about was what counts as evidence or how you obtain evidence or what to do with all of the other evidence that exists that you do not use.

To explore these questions, we returned to the story and I focused the students' attention on several passages that I consider key, in the sense of both salience and the ability to unlock. The examples I have chosen are not the only important ones in the text, just the ones I have found most useful to illustrate how readings, both my own and those of students, are constructed.

KEY 1

"I'm Mrs. Concord," Helen's mother said.

"I'm Mrs. Friedman," Mrs. Friedman said. "Bob Friedman's mother."

"Bob Friedman," Mrs. Concord repeated."

Mrs. Friedman smiled apologetically. "I thought surely your boy would have mentioned Bobby," she said. (193)

The surnames Concord and Friedman are repeated more than sixty times in a story of twelve hundred words. Some students took this to be a sign that the author is needlessly repetitive. I asked them to consider why a professional writer, who obviously has an extensive vocabulary and certainly knows how to use pronouns, would compose in this manner. Of course, such repetition from an accomplished writer means pay attention. The identity that those surnames encode and the lack of first-name familiarity between the women promise to be crucial aspects of the story. Over the years, my students, largely African Caribbean in Brooklyn at Medgar Evers College or European American in rural Pennsylvania at Penn State, usually have not connected the surnames to a contrast between Anglo-Saxon Protestants and Jews. The connection is readily apparent to me because I was raised in New York City and attended schools with major Jewish populations. I had a Friedman in my class, along with Goldbergs and Rosens and others, for twelve consecutive years. My students suggest that not every Friedman in the United States is Jewish, a proposition I concede whether I know it to be true or not. The point is that I tend to *read* Friedman as Jewish because of experience and knowledge I have that seem pertinent to the case. One could choose to insist on another reading of Friedman. But should one? Some of the students from the particular class in question locked in on the semantic marker *dark* and constructed Mrs. Friedman as African American. They read *dark* in terms of a black-white binary and not as a descriptor sometimes employed to distinguish phenotype among white ethnics. I let them go. I intended to demonstrate what I consider to be a cogent interpretation, but I was not out to suppress all others. My main point, and students quickly grasped this, is that one's response to language is never neutral, innocent, or obvious—nor is that language.

KEY 2

Helen went to answer the door. She opened it and stood smiling while the woman outside held out a hand and began to talk rapidly. "You're Helen? I'm Mrs. Friedman," she said. "I hope you won't think I'm just breaking in on you, but I have been so anxious to meet you and your mother."

"How do you do?" Helen said. "Won't you come in?" She opened the door wider and Mrs. Friedman stepped in. She was small and dark and wearing a very smart leopard coat. (193)

Concerning this passage, students, growing more attentive to language, generally have more to say about *dark* as race. The leopard coat sometimes confounds them, however, because for them it indicates a higher social class for Mrs. Friedman and makes her an unlikely target of prejudice. I asked my most recent students what they made of the fact that the author does not indicate that Helen accepts Mrs. Friedman's extended hand. Is that a writer's oversight? After all, an author does not present every possible detail. Maybe the author just doesn't do handshakes.

Key 3

"Well," Helen said, "I know that Bob got you a Japanese sword for Christmas. *That* must have looked lovely under the tree." (194–95)

If students are with me so far, they'll see the insensitivity in Helen's remark about Christmas, which Mrs. Friedman would not have been observing in a religious sense. What is most important here is to indicate how this anecdote is a rich contribution to one pattern of meaning and much less interesting if one is not aware of that pattern.

Key 4

"Well, Charlie certainly thinks a lot of his family," Mrs. Friedman said. "Wasn't he nice to write me?" she asked Helen.

"That tobacco must be good," Helen said. She hesitated for a minute and handed the letter back to Mrs. Friedman, who put it in her purse. (195)

Not much needs to be said by this juncture in class. The idea that the story is full of empty banter or mere chitchat has long been dispelled. The students saw that Helen willfully ignores Mrs. Friedman's question. But still no unanimity existed about why. Some resented what they saw as Mrs. Friedman's condescension and read Helen's actions, as well as those of her mother, sympathetically. I didn't spend a lot of time on the matter. It was on to the next key.

KEY 5

"I hope it won't be long now," Mrs. Friedman said. All three were silent for a minute, and then Mrs. Friedman went on with animation, "It seems so strange that we've been living in the same town and it took our boys so far away to introduce us."

"This is a very hard town to get acquainted in," Mrs. Concord said.

"Have you lived here long?" Mrs. Friedman smiled apologetically. "Of course I know of your husband," she added. "My sister's children are in your husband's high school and they speak so highly of him."

"Really?" Mrs. Concord said. "My husband has lived here all his life. I came here from the West when I was married."

"Then it hasn't been hard for you to get settled and make friends," Mrs. Friedman said.

"No, I never had much trouble," Mrs. Concord said. "Of course most of my friends are people who went to school with my husband." (195–96)

Mrs. Friedman gains fans. Here I gained a few more students willing to entertain anti-Semitism as a theme, if not necessarily *the* theme. Mrs. Concord claims that the town is hard one in which to get acquainted unless you are like a Concord. I had less and less to say.

KEY 6

"Give Bob our best regards when you write him," Helen said.

"I will," Mrs. Friedman said. "I'll tell him all about meeting you. It's been very nice," she said, holding out her hand to Mrs. Concord.

"I've enjoyed it," Mrs. Concord said. (197)

No one missed that Mrs. Friedman's hand is again extended. And no one thought the author has simply omitted the detail of a following handshake. The dominant idea in class was that there is no handshake. Both Mrs. Concord and her daughter are inclined to keep things old, Satterthwaite & Harris old.

No doubt, I influenced the responses of most of my students, but I did not dictate them. We were as much engaged in negotiation and deliberation as they had been in their smaller groups. It's just that as an old head I was able to bring more to the game, a fact they appreciated. To lead, to teach, were exactly my aim and responsibility. In the process, by valuing their input and fading into the background on occasion, I tried to stay in league with Lazere and West and their Emersonian vision, while trying to avoid the "narration sickness" that Freire cites as a major educational problem (57). As West put it, "To speak then of an Emersonian culture of creative democracy is to speak of a society and culture where politically adjudicated forms of knowledge are produced in which human participation is encouraged and for which human personalities are enhanced" (*American Evasion of Philosophy* 213).

I don't get much opportunity actually to measure personality enhancement, but I do get to observe the development of more mature approaches to language and argument. In my "Theories of Reading and Writing" course, students read, discuss, and report on texts such as McChesney and John Nichols's *Our Media Not Theirs*, Louise Rosenblatt's *The Reader, The Text, The Poem*, Gordon M. Pradl's *Literature for Democracy*, Paul Heilker's *Essay*, and Romy Clark and Roz Ivanič's *Politics of Writing*. In "Rhetorical Traditions," they may handle Lakoff's *Language War*, Michelle Hall Kells, Valerie Balester, and Victor Villanueva's *Latino/a Discourses*, John Russell Rickford and Russell John Rickford's *Spoken Soul*, and Morris Young's *Minor Re/Visions*. Participants in "Rhetoric and Composition," a course for first-year students, sample shorter texts by a number of writers, including Richard Rodriguez, Amy Tan, Lisa Kanae, Jamaica Kincaid, Deborah Tannen, Camille Paglia, Barbara Ehrenreich, Bharati Mukherjee, Kenneth Stampp, and Lani Guinier. Often eschewing the knee-jerk or absolute reads, or at least reflecting on them, the students become more and more attuned, as West would put it, to "the social and communal circumstances under which persons can communicate and cooperate in the process of acquiring knowledge" (*American Evasion of Philosophy* 213). They become more dialogic and unquiet, as Freire would envision them, as would current composition practitioners like Patricia Stock (*The Dialogic Curriculum*) and Eleanor Kutz and Hephzibah Roskelly (*An Unquiet Pedagogy*). They would earn the Good Socratic Seal from West.

The Promise of Odyssey

In Langston Hughes's "Theme for English B," the poetic persona recounts being told by his instructor at City College in New York.

Go home and write
a page tonight.
And let that page come out of you—
Then, it will be true.

(409)

The student wonders if the assignment can be that simple given cultural variances, geographical differences, political realities, and individual characteristics, including his own age, twenty-two, when much appears uncertain. But, in a phenomenological move, he suggests to himself that he is what he feels, sees, and hears, and he understands that the page is a site of transaction between himself and his surroundings. Our dutiful student, struggling toward truth—"It's not easy to know what is true for you or me"—reflects on some of his own tastes, considers commonalties and differences among races, and ponders the idea of American identity (409).

Well, I like to eat, sleep, drink, and be in love.
I like to work, read, learn, and understand life.
I like a pipe for a Christmas present,
or records—Bessie, bop, or Bach.
I guess being colored doesn't make me not like
the same things other folks like who are other races.
So will my page be colored that I write?
Being me, it will not be white.
But it will be
A part of you, instructor.
You are white—
Yet a part of me, as I am a part of you.
That's American.

(410)

Our student writer then muses further upon the interdependence as well as conflict that American identity entails, acknowledging that neither students like him nor people like the instructor always want to be caught in the same web but that the web is inescapable. Given the ties, the student reasons, he and the instructor learn from each other, even if the instructor is "older—and white—and somewhat more free" (410). As he notes his final point, or discovery, he announces in seeming triumph, "This is my page for English B" (410).

This poem provokes much discussion among writing instructors. In 2003, Kathleen Yancey chose the title to be the theme of the annual convention of the Conference on College Composition and Communication. More than three thousand compositionists gathered in New York City to discuss college writing, and much attention was devoted to what students like the poetic persona have achieved. Over the years, I have heard far less about the instructor, though I have thought of him or her often. Who issued the generative command to "let that page come out of you"? Did that professor, for example, anticipate the outcome? Did he or she know that "come out of" was the directive that would trigger an examination of the relationship between the individual and society? Why did he or she have such faith in such instruction? Was the assignment just impulsive or part of a reflective, elaborate plan about how teachers and students should proceed in English B? I like to imagine that it was a plan by that teacher, which means, of course, that it is a pedagogical statement by Hughes, maybe the articulation of a Bessie, bop, and Bach pedagogy, a formula with an expressivist pop worthy of Peter Elbow but with enough critical content to gesture toward the social-epistemic rhetoric of Jim Berlin and the Socratic commitment espoused by West.

The instructor's directive in "Theme for English B" also connects with the Odyssey Project, a writing initiative in which I participated at Syracuse University. A late 1980s brainchild of Patricia Stock and carried forward by the likes of Louise Wetherbee Phelps, Nance Hahn, Faith Plvan, and (later) me, the project viewed literacy, literacy learning, and literacy assessment as activities that inform one another. Therefore, an ambitious effort was made to integrate these processes in a pedagogical and research design intended to map and analyze the writing development of students over the period of a decade. What the project more modestly became, beginning in 1991, was a series of progressive writing courses, extracurricular activities, and in-service teacher development moments that still influence how I teach today.

Essential to the Odyssey approach was prodding students to become self-reflective about their literacy journey, about how they came to learn *and learn through* language. Toward this end, in the first-year writing course, they were assigned to write literacy autobiographies the aim of which was not to reconstitute the past, an impossibility, but to recover a version of the past that could clarify their challenges in the present and for the future. As James Olney remarks about this sort of endeavor, "Memory issues in and validates present being because it is simultaneously a tracing that leads to present consciousness; it integrates all the old, half-remembered, or perhaps misremembered, selves, which were adequate to their own proper moments, into patterns of the new self, which is born in the moment now out of this very exercise of consciousness and memory" (264–65). In addition to the strategic value to be derived from student self-reflection about literacy, Odyssey instructors felt that student literacy autobiographies represented a markedly democratic feature of the writing curriculum. Each student voice would be heard and each set of experiences valued. Room for the essay, in the exploring sense of Michel Montaigne and Langston Hughes, would be made. Everyone's self-interrogation, knowledge, and style would matter. The very vitality of the envisioned classroom, which we called writing studios to stress their participatory nature, depended on the breadth and depth of such student involvement. Instructors emphasized collaboration and the building of intellectual communities. Students were given books to read such as Mike Rose's *Lives on the Boundary*, Annie Dillard's *An American Childhood*, Jill Kerr Conway's *Road from Coorain*, Villanueva's *Bootstraps*, Richard Rodriguez's *Hunger of Memory* (I never agreed with him but never discriminated against him), and my own *Voices of the Self*. For better or worse, I was the Odyssey experiment carried to its logical conclusion. I recall one of my students writing, "Oh, what a life of iniquity this young man led," when I never thought I was all that bad (well, sometimes). At any rate, students were able to see that the self-reflective writing asked of them had gained respectability in the academic and publishing worlds. They also were given the chance to weigh in as critics and further establish intellectual authority. Student selections were included in a reader that Nance, Faith, and I eventually compiled for Odyssey courses. Other students were scheduled to work as compensated researchers as part of the proposed longitudinal study. They would become "researching subjects," not merely the subjects of research. Most important, they would be developing language awareness, facility, and power to be used in a myriad of contexts both in and beyond school.

After they produced literacy autobiographies, students were required to conduct ethnographic study of language practices—usually in a dorm, student center, or classroom—and produce a critical paper. The general point was to deal, as Phillip Lopate suggests, critically with the *I*. The Odyssey Project valued student voices but not static ones. We had too much respect for students not to believe that their perspectives could be sharpened, deepened, and made more sophisticated while remaining theirs, the products of their intellectual labor. The democratic impulse requires that the collective body *keep* deliberating.

To prepare for their ethnographic research, students were given model ethnographic texts, such as, Andrea Fishman's *Amish Literacy*. Early in the program, Fishman accepted an invitation to visit campus, where she conducted a workshop and held two question-and-answer sessions for students. In general, students worked enthusiastically on their ethnographies, finding it difficult sometimes to make the familiar strange, a habit of mind for language scholars, but also discovering new excitement when they began to discern patterns. As pioneering instructor Faith Plvan observes, "Ethnographic work demanded that they begin to see themselves as scholars because it required that they intellectualize about 'ordinary' things as they took on the role of key worker in the research process" (3). Usually, when the students finished their ethnographies, they were only then ready to *really* begin. But this was no less true of Fishman, who, after showing her dissertation director hundreds of pages of work, was told that she was then ready to commence. Unfortunately, the semester didn't allow time for a second ethnography, though one could pursue further ethnographic study as part of the overall research initiative. But students drew on their ethnographies as well as their literacy autobiographies, the class readings, and whatever other materials they obtained to write their final major assignment, a critical paper on some aspect of language or literacy, which required in practical terms a reevaluation of ideas encountered and developed over the course of the semester.

Obviously, I found great value in Odyssey. I was particularly intrigued, for example, that the project held special appeal for so-called minority students. When extracurricular events like workshops, panels, and film showings were organized, these students, from a group that was less than 15 percent of the university population, would typically constitute more than 50 percent of the audience. They also were overrepresented among those who volunteered to do research. Psychologist Claude M. Steele helped Odyssey instructors think explicitly about what was represented implicitly in the curriculum. In a 1992 article in *Atlantic Monthly*, "Race and the Schooling of Black Americans," Steele proposed the notion of "disidentification," a detached pose some African American students effected on predominately white campuses to lessen the impact of racial insult or discrimination. Their pose was racial armor that in their minds allowed them to combat racial devaluing. It was readily evident, and Steele suggested as much, that educational initiatives that valued the personal experiences of African American students, assigned importance to their viewpoints, and depended on their contributions to collaborative enterprises, were effective measures to thwart psychic alienation.[4]

Because I have worked at predominately white institutions over the second half of my career, I stay attuned to possible instances of disidentification by so-called minority students. But I also remain enthused about what Odyssey offered all students. Plvan stated the case, based on student evaluations, as well as anyone in her 1993 talk at CCCC.

> They had these things to say in their reflective essays and course evaluations. Most had little difficulty staying interested in the course. The exploration of literacy motivated them, and the way the three major writing assignments connected sustained this motivation. They characterized their work as portable, purposeful, and goal-oriented, and they talked about ways they were already using what they learned in this class in their other classes. By the end of the semester, they described themselves as more confident, flexible, adaptable, versatile writers. They knew themselves better, they were tuned in to their individual strengths and weaknesses, and they had relished what one student called the "rare opportunity to study myself and my writing." They had fun learning to know themselves better—the literacy autobiography usually called up fond memories, memories that as first-semester freshmen, they were often happy to recall and savor. They took pride in what I would describe as the realization that they were becoming adults who were now able to reflect on and categorize various aspects of their childhood lives. Nance [Nance Hahn] told me that many of her students liked calling home to "research" this assignment. The frequent peer interaction and the regular conferences helped them make friends and eased their entry into a new academic conversation and a new intellectual community. The collaborative classroom and the pleasure of belonging to a community also supported them as they worked to meet the rigorous challenges of the class. (6–7)

Odyssey, then, was one learning community's successful, Socratic response to a Freirean call for critical literacy or heightened language awareness. The experiment was grounded in principles of dialogism and democracy and relied fundamentally upon student input. We probably should have pushed more on the topic of language. This would strike some as an odd comment given that language was the express topic of Odyssey courses, too much so in the opinion of some. But we could have benefited from a genealogical-materialist approach of the sort suggested by Michel Foucault and also practiced by West.

Genealogies, in the sense that West employs them, do not simply trace what occurred. They are also concerned with how and why things occurred, what that occurrence precluded, and the impact of these developments on subjectivity. This is not to deprivilege agency, at least not in my view, or to make a hard social-constructionist turn. We have no choice in the physical and social beings we initially become, but once we become physical and social beings, we certainly have choices to make. We are indeed produced but not completed. Yet, in Odyssey, we insufficiently theorized the social production of literacy. A genealogical approach enables one to better analyze literacy narratives and improve one's own.

Although personnel changes and inadequate funding compromised the project over the long haul, strands of Odyssey exist in current composition courses, including my own. For example, for a recent first-year composition course that by special designation also satisfied the "United States Cultures" requirement, I specified that language variation would be a focus of the course along with race, ethnicity, gender, and class. I had students write literacy narratives but not ones as lengthy and detailed as those produced by Odyssey students. However, I coaxed them to talk about why some of their language habits formed in one way as opposed to some possible alternative. One student responded:

> In my own experience with my family, many situations required me to know more than one language. I was born to my parents who were both immigrants from Hungary. My father knew enough English in order to function in everyday life in America. His knowledge of English allowed him to obtain a job which caused him to work long hours each day. My mother, on the other hand, had absolutely no knowledge of English. In the schools my mother attended as a girl in Hungary, no English language classes were offered. She stayed home with me during my infancy while my father, the English-speaker, was not present. The first words I spoke were not English, but Hungarian taught by my mother who could only speak that language. It was not until I learned how to work the

television set that I began learning English from programs such as *Sesame Street*, *Mr. Rogers*, and others.

With enough time and guidance, the student could have examined the genealogical angle more fully, maybe investigated why her father's language experiences in Hungary differed from her mother's, circumstances that had a direct impact on her own language development. She completed a mini-Odyssey course. Along with mining her personal experience, she wrote about her observations of others, mainly with regard to the issues of monolingualism and bilingualism. In addition, she wrote critically about language policy.

A second sample from the course, a response to Lani Guinier's "Tyranny of the Majority" is also about language but not in the sense that we would have discussed it in Odyssey. By far, Guinier's essay provoked the most-spirited reactions, positive and negative, expressed by students that semester. I did not expect this development, but in retrospect I understand that Guinier, of all the writers we read, most disrupted a dominant and largely invisible discourse, that is, the nexus of ideology, language, and historical consciousness inside which majority rule in the nation is regarded as an unquestioned and unquestionable assumption. Recalling Lakoff, we understand that for my students, "majority rule" occupied the unmarked rhetorical position. Why would anyone dare argue, some wondered, that our current system of voting is not always the best solution to policy disagreements in our culture? Lakoff comments on Guinier's demonstration of Socratic commitment, "We get upset and angry when the relationship between frames and reality is challenged. That may explain the ease with which Lani Guinier's proposal for proportional voting was challenged and disposed of, and the ease with which she was tarred with the epithet 'quota queen'" (50).

Guinier draws on her own personal experience, select scenarios, and her reading of history to challenge nonetheless. For example, Guinier cites the case of high school students in Chicago who held two senior proms. The African American seniors, a numerical minority, knew that they could never win a vote concerning the music to be featured; therefore, they organized an alternate affair, a move that left some of the white students at the school embittered because they felt that majority rule is the "way it works" and that the African Americans should have abided by the vote (609). Guinier argues that both groups were correct in their thinking: "From the white students' perspective, this was ordinary decision making. To the black students, majority rule sent the message: 'we don't count' is the 'way it works' for minorities'" (609). Thus, Guinier moves on to one of her central points: "In a racially divided society, majority rule may be perceived as majority tyranny" (609). Guinier has read intently the political writings from the early years of our republic, particularly those of James Madison, who worried about the power that a firmly consolidated, fixed, or permanent majority could wield in a heterogeneous society. Guinier proffers a "principle of taking turns" with one major salutary effect: "Because those with 51 percent of the vote are not assured 100 percent of the power, the majority cooperates with, or at least does not tyrannize, the minority. . . . I do not believe that democracy should encourage rule by the powerful—even a powerful majority" (611–12).

In the face of this unfamiliar theory, this radically new frame, students had to decide whether they could embrace or defend what they considered at first glance to be such an unorthodox stance. Although no student was required to write about Guinier's essay—other choices were available—the majority (not a tyrannical one) did. And some supported her, which either suggests (I'm glad) that frames operate with far less than Whorfian impact or that another frame kicked in that had to do with appreciating fundamental fairness. One example of support:

> Voting is often thought of as a fair and accurate way to listen to the people and give them what they want. However, in many cases basing decisions solely on the majority can upset other people whose opinions aren't valued. I learned of this unfairness in voting during my high school years where the minority was often forgotten about because they were not part of the majority. My physics and math tests, more often than not, fell on the same day throughout the year. Our physics teacher would allow our class to vote whether or not we wanted the date to be switched. However, the majority of the class was enrolled in a different math class than me and the other students. While we were constantly voting to have the date of the exam changed, they always opted to keep it on the same day. Since they were the majority, the tests were never changed for the better of the minority.
>
> Quickly, I realized the unfairness of this voting. The minority's voices were never going to be heard since the changes were based on voting every time. The majority seemed to think that this was a fair

way to determine it because the majority was fixed and people were not switching sides. No compromise was ever made. This is a common issue when it comes to voting in governments and those who fall under that minority category often feel cheated. The majority may not represent the whole and, therefore, the minority's opinion is very rarely valued in a government with a majority tyranny.

Conducting a government in this manner causes many more conflicts than conducting a classroom in this way, but the ideas parallel each other. In the classroom, the minority quickly become annoyed and frustrated with this situation and many started bribing the majority to have them vote our way. This is a common occurrence in government voting as well. The minority quickly becomes restless and feels they are being cheated from a democracy. This group attempts to convert the majority to their side. Conducting such a win-lose situation like those seen in sports always cheats one group of what they want or need.

Carrying out a majority tyranny in what should be a democracy makes sense when only one group can win. However, the idea of democracy is to have fair and equal voting for all people and, therefore, this way of ruling and decision making is not reasonable. This form of government should mean taking turns and discussing ways to compromise and meet every person's goals and aspirations for the country. Going back to what happened in my physics classroom, it is easy to see from an outsider's point of view that a compromise should have been made in order to maintain happiness within the classroom. The minority became alienated because of the fixed vote every time.

The assumption that the majority represents the minority may be true in some homogenous societies. However, this is not the case for most societies because people usually have conflicting interests and ideas concerning different topics of debate. Those who make up the majority do not see the flaw in this way of voting and do not show interest in the minority's point of view. This stubbornness does not allow compromise to be made.

Majority tyranny is not a reasonable form of government because where it is present, there is no genuine democracy. It becomes an unchanging and predetermined vote that excludes the minority every time. Only the majority will have a say in every election and every vote on issues within the nation. With the tyranny, the minority will be quickly forgotten.

This is not the polished version it could be with more work. The immediate point I want to make is that the student brought forward bothersome episodes from her own past that she could examine in a new light given the writing of Guinier, whose disruption of dominant discourse enabled the student's similar opposition to a common sense, prevailing, exnominated "regime of truth." I would have preferred the student to indicate how her thinking on the matter diverged from Guinier's at some point, if only just a little. No one should capitulate totally to the professionals they read. But the student's example is as compelling as those of Guinier. It's her life. Besides, I have been in the audience listening to Guinier. She can be quite persuasive.

A Rival Hypothesis, or Socratic Commitment *Plus*

No one in composition studies has made a more systematic attempt to incorporate the insights of Cornel West into his or her teaching and scholarship than Linda Flower. With colleagues Elenore Long and Lorraine Higgins, Flower has developed and researched the concept of *rival hypothesis stance* (RHS), or rivaling, defined as an "important literate practice in which people explore open questions through an analysis of multiple perspectives" (4). Rivaling is a method of collaborative, intercultural inquiry informed largely by John Dewey's pragmatism and West's prophetic response to those ideas. As the authors assert in *Learning to Rival*, "The prophetic pragmatism of Cornel West—and its demand for a 'strong' version of the rival hypothesis stance—challenges us to construct a representation of 'others' that can name social and material structures of power and domination, at the same time that it boldly acknowledges the agency of marginalized others and invokes action" (12). Flower and her colleagues, while working primarily with pre-college African American students on campus and a group of urban teenagers in a community setting, have attempted nothing short of translating prophetic pragmatism into what they term a "prophetic rhetoric," a flexible, instructive, learner-centered, but nonreplicable-in-detail process of questioning and knowing—in the general pragmatist tradition—inflected with West's sense of political urgency (20). And by strong rival hypothesis stance, Flower herself means a version of rivaling that "recognizes radical differences in interpretation and significance given your cultural position, as well as the possibility of incommensurate perspectives" ("Rival Hypothesis Stance" 47). As such, the project of strong rivaling echoes West's critique of Dewey. It also relates to Socratic commitment—but goes beyond a strict association with the method of Socrates. Flower is aware of Bertrand Russell's contention that Socratic dialogue fails as a method for generating knowledge but functions instead as an arbiter of problems about which we have sufficient information but to which we have insufficiently applied the rules of logic (35). In "An Experimental Way of Knowing," she alludes to Socrates' practice of disputation in Plato's *Phaedrus*, and she eventually concludes, "In a Socratic dialogue one often suspects not all rivals are genuine options" (49).

Yet, critique of oppressive power brokers is in the work of Socrates, as West points out. In addition, West's recommendation of Socratic commitment comes with a prophetic-pragmatist exhortation to relentlessly explore intellectual matters and contest injustice in practical terms. As a discursive strategy, strong rivaling really is (as are the ideas of West that helped to give it shape) Socratic commitment *plus*—disputation, frank questioning of power, and a quest for action agendas. This is perhaps more accurate nomenclature for a discursive strategy used to surge toward solutions, however contingent, for complex personal, social, and educational problems.

Steady on the Case

Critical literacy is thoroughly entwined with Socratic commitment (*plus*) of the type promoted by West and Flower. A number of composition instructors have both anticipated and heard West when he argues, "The democratic energies of Socratic questioning tend to brazenly and forcefully challenge the corrupt rule of elites and often subject its practitioners to ridicule and censure of various kinds. Yet Socratic questioning is indispensable to any democratic experiment . . . Without Socratic questioning by the demos, elite greed at home and imperial domination abroad devour any democracy" (*Democracy Matters* 209, 211). Pondering a genealogical tracing that encompasses Freirean liberatory gestures and an Emersonian democratic vision, West expounds upon the origins of Athenian democracy, the challenge of Socrates to the greed and corruption of the Sophists, and Socrates' educational method, particularly as reflected in dialogues like *Apology* and *Meno*. He considers Socrates' pronouncement in *Apology* that choosing good over bad is more important than preferring life over death (14) and his expert tutelage of the slave boy in *Meno* (365–70). Many of us, however, would view the lesson through Deweyan and Freirean lenses. From this perspective, the slave boy did not, as Socrates claimed, retrieve principles of geometry that already existed in his soul. He brought physical and social tools to the process. Without him being sighted, fluent in Greek (which Socrates ascertained beforehand), and in command of the linguistic-mathematical concepts *half* and *twice*, the lesson could not have transpired. With those tools to process the information encoded in Socrates' questions, the boy, in conjunction with Socrates, fashioned knowledge and solved or "named the answer" to the geometry puzzle.

But whatever our pedagogical position, the general point concerning critique and dialogic inquiry is well taken. Our students may not "out-Socratize Socrates," as West proposes they do, but we hope they pursue the examined life with gusto, develop relentless critical facility, retain intellectual integrity, commit to the never-ending pursuit of genuine democracy, and speak forthrightly when they know it is time to do so (*Democracy Matters* 213). It is the best that composition instructors, in the role of composition instructors, can promote.

4

Tracking Prophetic Witness

FLOWING FROM a wellspring of deep democratic energies, prophetic witness, according to Cornel West, "consists of human deeds of justice and kindness that attend to the unjust sources of human hurt and misery. It calls attention to the causes of unjustified suffering and unnecessary social misery and highlights personal and institutional evil, including the evil of being indifferent to personal and institutional evil" (*Democracy Matters* 114). Such strategy, therefore, complements and extends the major aim of critical composition practices, which also focus on analyses of oppression, usually as related to race, gender, and class, and mainly through close inspections of discourse. Naturally, evocations of prophecy conjure up visions of the religious, generally a suspect topic or pose to rationalist pedagogues (including me). Nonetheless, in recent years, compelling cases have been made by composition scholars to suggest that faith issues should be a crucial area of investigation in rhetorical education. This chapter outlines this argument and its connection to West's notion of prophetic witness. In addition, I consider several related ideas, including the relationships among prophetic witness, race, class, and the work of Michel Foucault.

Faith Matters

Theorist bell hooks reports that her academic training encouraged her to refrain from discussions of spirituality and religion in the classroom. But such advice was at odds with her instincts and felt experience. As she recalls in *Teaching Community*, "Certainly, coming from a segregated black world where claiming spiritual identity had been a place of critical resistance, a way to stand against racist dehumanization, I valued spiritual life" (179). Furthermore, taking a broader and longer view, she concludes, "The movement from slavery to freedom, sexism to feminism, discrimination to greater openness . . . all these incredible movements for social justice succeeded when they evoked an ethic of love rooted in the embrace of spirit" (183). As a Stanford undergraduate, hooks often found sanctuary in the campus church as she grappled with the discomforts of her journey from segregated Kentucky to the halls of elite academe. She now believes that the possibilities for such solace should not be left to the individual wanderings of students, especially if they feel marginalized within college or university environs. Rather than considering classroom concern with spirituality to be anti-intellectual, she believes that rigorous scrutiny of spiritual issues is a necessary component of any work she does as a teacher. Helping students to become whole, hooks suggests, works against the status quo, and she offers herself as a model: "Honestly naming spirituality as a force strengthening my capacity to resist enabled me to stand within centers of dominator culture and courageously offer alternatives" (181). For her, therefore, "The classroom continues to be a place where paradise can be realized, a place of passion and possibility, a place where spirit matters, where all that we learn and know leads us into greater connection, into greater understanding of life lived in community" (183).

Although spirituality and religion are not synonymous for hooks, the former focusing on the health of the human spirit without a requisite adherence to ecclesiastical doctrine, in practical terms the two concepts often blend for students. A great majority of American college students profess belief in some religion, and, as Bradford T. Stull indicates, "If American discourse is nothing else, it is an attempt to weave sociopolitical and religious language into a seamless garment that would clothe us" (18). "America as the New Israel" and "America as Eden" resonate powerfully as metaphors in the nation's imagination. One of the most famous speeches in American history,

Martin Luther King Jr.'s "I Have a Dream" oration, plays skillfully on this. Stull reminds us that although King announces that his dream is rooted in the American dream, the two visions are overlapping and not coterminous. King ranges beyond the American democratic notion of enlightened citizens intelligently debating and solving problems. Instead, he sees, in Stull's view, a "profound communion of landscape and human polity and God" (116). Although less discussed, King's second "dream speech," his 1967 "A Christmas Sermon on Peace," does not gesture to American roots or focus on current American society.[1] This King is internationalist and Edenic in his outlook, or, in Stull's words, "The natural realm is itself healed, with antagonists like the lamb and the lion transformed into companions, even comrades, sharing space peacefully, without rancor, bloodshed, death" (119). Referring to additional King comments and metaphors about the cessation of war, the glory of God, and the Edenic vision, Stull adds, "So, too, humans having beat their swords into plowshares, their spears into pruning hooks, having, in short, become gardeners, find themselves at home in the natural order. No longer battling over land, no longer afraid, they rest under vines and figs" (119).[2]

Of course, any discussion of King in relation to composition studies could hardly avoid mention of "Letter from Birmingham City Jail," the text of his that is most anthologized in college readers and most discussed and written about in composition courses. Although emphasis is usually placed on King's rhetorical—and intellectual—acumen, an essential quality of the text is that it is pitched from preacher to clergymen, steeped in a language that they all are presumed to share.

Mindful of how religion is often teased out of ruminations about theory, Ann Berthoff posed a question at the 1988 CCCC, in a panel addressing Paulo Freire's politics and pedagogy, about why no one paid due attention to his religious beliefs and commentary about churches given that Freire was a major proponent of liberation theology and drew distinctions among the traditional church unconcerned with modern social problems, the liberal church, which contributed good will and technical assistance, and the prophetic church concerned with political, cultural, and personal transformation. Although no satisfactory response was forthcoming on that occasion, in 1992, Berthoff joined Beth Daniell, JoAnn Campbell, C. Jan Swearingen, and James Moffett for a CCCC presentation titled "Sites of Spiritual Composing." Revised remarks from that panel were published in *College Composition and Communication* in 1994. For example, Berthoff suggested:

The idea of the prophetic church can awaken us to the root meaning of *religion* as binding force. And it offers a powerful antidote to the new positivism, which is called "antifoundationalism," a variant of context-free ideology. The point is not to discard foundations, which it is logically impossible to do anyway, but to examine them with a critical consciousness. *Spirit* is a very powerful speculative instrument for this enterprise." (238)

We might press Berthoff on her claim that antifoundationalism functions as the new positivism or on how she construes thinking that is all about context to be context-free. Nonetheless, she is correct in her judgment that religion is an attractive heuristic for many composition students.

Indeed, in *Collision Course*, Russell K. Durst notes that students at the University of Cincinnati frequently opted to write about religion when asked to write about group membership relative to prejudice and diversity. Religion was perceived to be the safe topic, less contentious and charged than issues of race and ethnicity (154). This observation runs counter to Anne Ruggles Gere's remark in *College English* that it is "much more acceptable to detail the trauma of rape or abuse than to recount a moment of religious inspiration" (Symposium Collective 47), words disputed by David L. Wallace, a queer scholar and former evangelical Christian. Wallace sympathizes with Gere's sense of erasure but claims that her comments do not interrogate the "considerable privilege that her Christianity allows her in American culture, tied as it often is to whiteness, professional-class membership and heterosexual markers" (504). In other words, Wallace understands that many folks get thrown to the lions in America but not whites *as whites*, men *as men*, or Christians *as Christians*. To be fair to Gere, and both Wallace and I fully intend to be, it must be noted that she is initially quoted out of context. She was composing an exploratory piece for a print symposium subtitled "The Politics of the Personal: Storying Our Lives against the Grain" and responding to a query by Gesa Kirsch and Min-Zhan Lu, who asked, "To what extent have your racial, gender, ethnic, sexual, religious, or class alignments complicated your response to the pressure/invitations to live and represent the personal within the confines of personal narrative?" (Symposium Collective 42). Gere was recounting her own experiences as a practicing Christian in academe and articulating the challenges she faced as she coauthored a memoir with her daughter, who introduced to her Native American spirituality. Before making the claim to which Wallace objects, Gere was bemoaning that in her view, "current norms of personal writing, shaped as they have been by the values of the academy, militate against writing about religious experience" (46–47). Shortly after making the assertion to which Wallace takes exception, Gere argues, "Those who wish to write about religion not only lack the highly complex and compelling language of, say, queer theory, but they confront an implacable secularism" (47). This still sounds like special pleading to me. All emerging areas of study have to fill linguistic voids, and Gere faces no barrier in that regard other than her own shortcomings. But Gere's ideas and Wallace's recent, and ultimately considerate, response to those musings, indicate that in composition studies the conversation about religion, already vibrant, will remain important, as Durst and others like Sharon Crowley suggest, in the foreseeable future.[3]

Amy Goodburn agrees that teachers ought to become better prepared for encounters with students who view religion as the source of their primary identities. Although she considers the dogma of Christian fundamentalism to be problematic and had a trying experience with a student bloc of Christian conservatives at Ohio State, she understands that rather than simply pronouncing disengagement with aspects of the everyday world, fundamentalism constitutes a method of social criticism in that a host of social and cultural activities are evaluated with respect to a strict, literal interpretive grid, not totally unlike the case with the application of other critical methods. Students like those she taught knew very well, as critical pedagogues would wish, that reading and writing are sociopolitical and that interpretation is context based. Goodburn contends, "In many ways, the responses of students with fundamentalist beliefs serve as a mirror (albeit some critical educators might suggest a dark one) that reflects the principles of critical pedagogy from a different location" (349). Goodburn ultimately suggests that critical pedagogues and fundamentalist students can find common ground in the language of critique and that perhaps a dose of "faith"—in the possibilities of dialogue and the reasonable negotiation of differences between students and teachers—is a crucial aspect of critical pedagogy (352). Similarly, Priscilla Perkins thinks that most teachers are too quickly dismissive of evangelical Christian students. In her class, she saw such students transcending "textophobia" and engaging in promising ways with James Baldwin's "Down at the Cross," Adrienne Rich's "Women and Honor: Some Notes on Lying," and Nawal el-Saadawi's "Love and Sex in the Life of the Arab" (601).

Lizabeth A. Rand also recognizes that religion may be a key component of the identities that students bring to class and may be the perspective from which they habitually confront the academy and world at large. She notes the suspicion of progressive, rationalist academics who relentlessly push their students toward objectivist discourse. Ironically, Rand declares, this teaching approach places emphasis on the subject position of the instructor, which violates a dictum verbally cherished by progressive educators: meet the students where they are. The problem, of course, lies in that instructors sometimes detest where the students are. But Rand argues that if we are serious about improving composition practice, then we must study more seriously the ways in which the religious dispositions of students inform composition classrooms. She feels that in the split between postmodern thought and religious belief, with most composition instructors, at least the more vocal ones, lined up on the side of the postmodern, evangelical Christians represent one particular group who are not served well. Aware that "witnessing talk" often rankles secular teachers, Rand asserts, like Goodburn, that parallels exist between such talk and leftist composition discourse, which itself verges on the evangelical. As she avers, "Compositionists call for students to 'lose' the notion of a unified self (ultimately oppressed because it is distracted from cultivating greater critical awareness) in order to 'find' the multiple and partial self (ideally liberated because it is conscious of the reality of social construction)" (360). According to Rand, radical composition instructors themselves act as witnesses trying to help students "get saved" (360). She plays out the metaphor further, "We typically argue that agency cannot be asserted until the self becomes reflexive enough to gain a 'sense of itself' as socially produced in and through language. Only then, it would follow, can one be set free or 'born again' in some sense: empowered to resist cultural codes that create suffering and alienation" (360–61).

With regard to specific practices, Rand suggests that students can conduct ethnographies of various religious subcultures and place their research within the context of wider public discourses. In the final analysis, she would caution instructors once again not to presume that evangelical discourse, in particular, is rhetorically unsophisticated or naïve. In not yielding to other authority, religion embodies a subversive character, according to Rand, and makes for expansive possibilities.

While Rand's criticism is powerful, I doubt that high-volume creativity is going to flow from fundamentalist or evangelical students. Their religiosity tends not to be of the prophetic, socially ameliorative type but the conservative, George W. Bush type. I have several friends in the profession trying to save my soul so they can deliver it to the Republican Party. I don't see how my soul could make it to heaven from there. While Rand pressures composition to examine the faultiness inherent in some of its prevailing constructs, she does not historicize the contrast between the fundamentalist and the prophetic and includes way too little assessment of the practical link between conservative Christianity and conservative political actions. Radical compositionists don't have a problem with Christian theorists per se; they wouldn't overwhelmingly embrace Cornel West if they did. They abhor the prominent role of conservative Christians in right-wing politics.

In the attempt to address productively the tensions between critical pedagogy and religion as well as to recognize more fully the points of intersection, Shari J. Stenberg's essay "Liberation Theology and Liberatory Pedagogies: Renewing the Dialogue" is most promising. Like Berthoff before her, she knows that Freire's roots in liberation theology are as consequential as his roots in Marxism and that blanket distrust of the spiritual compromises Freire's legacy (271). As she writes, "Scholars such as David Purpel and Svi Shapiro, Cornel West, and [Barry] Kanpol contend that it is exactly this lack of focus on the ethical and moral that has prevented the left from actualizing its visions" (277). Stenberg draws a distinction between the transformative intellectual and the prophetic teacher. The former aligns unwaveringly with a tradition of criticism geared to social change; the latter is also radically critical, respects the tradition of the former but stresses, in dealing with students, compassion, solidarity, and continual reflection and adjustment concerning pedagogy (283–84). Like Goodburn and Rand, among others, Stenberg knows that spirituality or religion for some students is the most important aspect of their self-identification. To her, prophetic teachers exploit the confluences of secular-critical and spiritual or religious projects. They don't dismiss notions of personal salvation or existential exploration, but they prod students to link selfhood to broader critical matters. "As Cornel West insists," she declares, "work in the prophetic tradition must be fueled by a 'sense of the larger context, the larger forces that shape and mold not only who we are but our projection of where we want to go'" (275).[4] Stenberg discerns in West's idea of "combative spirituality"—an outlook that deals with politics as well as with personal anxieties about death or despair—a way for composition instructors in particular to implement critical pedagogy more completely (287–89).[5]

If Donald McCrary is an accurate indication, African American composition teachers (in the manner of bell hooks) spend little time justifying the use of theological discourse in the classroom. The prophetic tradition has been so central to their people's historical struggle and progress in the United States that they assume its relevance and generative potential as pedagogy. McCrary asserts that he never would advocate for a particular religion in class, but as he worked in an urban school populated predominately by women of color and sought to "locate an active discourse community that would represent the language and culture of both my students and the academy while offering a hermeneutic that was compelling and liberating," he found just the ticket in womanist theology (527). McCrary used texts by figures such as Delores Williams, Jacquelyn Grant, Susan Hagood Lee, Ada Maria Isasi-Diaz, Chandra Taylor Smith, and Susan Johnson Smith, texts he understood to be collectively a stirring critique of racism, sexism, and class exploitation. These writings proved to be compelling to his students as well, who wrote a number of exemplary critical papers in response. McCrary attributes some of the technical progress that students made to their heightened engagement with the material. He felt that by using womanist theology, he located his students "in a sociohistorical position of importance" and worked in line with the critical project of providing students with "an accessible discourse and hermeneutic that challenges and critiques oppressive rhetoric both inside and outside the academy and that helps students to generate a rhetoric of their own that illustrates their competence as transcultural thinkers and writers" (549). He remains vitally concerned that students grasp the "ideological power behind interpretation, including the power of the knowing interpreter to inscribe subjectivity and centrality" (549–50).

Naturally, Cornel West endorses teaching projects, like McCrary's, that are firmly connected to the prophetic tradition in Christianity. But as he speaks to composition, he makes a more far-reaching, in-depth, and direct analysis of the issues at stake than composition scholars have advanced. He argues, "The battle for the soul of American democracy is, in large part, a battle for the soul of American Christianity, because the dominant forms of Christian fundamentalism are a threat to the tolerance and openness necessary for sustaining any democracy" (*Democracy Matters* 146). In line with his radical historicist leanings, West sketches a story, one from which Rand can benefit, of how political developments led to the formation of two basic categories of Christianity, the Constantinian and the prophetic. The former originated in the fourth century A.D. when the Roman emperor Constantine incorporated Christian doctrine into the empire. As a result, West contends, Christianity lost much of its prophetic fervor, and, in his view, the Constantinian variety has been used ever since to rationalize imperial aims all over the globe. In an American context, for example, Constantinian Christianity has been on the wrong side of issues like slavery and equal rights for women. West feels that Constantinian Christians, who focus on "personal conversion, individual piety, and philanthropic service," tend to respond to social issues by rallying around the flag and the cross, no matter how imperial the flag or how strongly the cross is aligned with injustice (*Democracy Matters* 150). Constantinian Christians (we know them more familiarly as the Religious Right) support militaristic foreign policy and oppose sufficient urban investment, proper funding of public education, and adequate responses to AIDS.

As a countering move, West, a highly public Christian, champions the prophetic history of Christianity and its concern with the downtrodden and social justice. He asserts in *The American Evasion of Philosophy* that his method of cultural criticism "invites all people of good will both here and abroad to fight for an Emersonian culture of creative democracy in which the plight of the wretched of the earth is alleviated" (235). Drawing on the Old Testament, he writes in *Democracy Matters*, "The prophetic figures in Israelite history—Jeremiah, Micah, Amos, Isaiah, and others—give voice to *divine* compassion and justice in order to awaken *human* compassion and justice" (114). West would have us all study the examples of Walter Rauschenbusch, Dorothy Day and the Catholic Worker Movement, Reverend William Sloan Coffin, Ida B. Wells-Barnett, David Walker, and, of course, Martin Luther King Jr.

In jostling for room in the public sphere, West has had to elbow not only with Constantinian Christians, though this is where much of the action is, but with liberals like John Rawls and anticlericalists like Richard Rorty, who would excise religious discourse from that domain (*Democracy Matters* 160–61). As Rorty argues in "Anticlericalism and Atheism," for example, "Religion is unobjectionable as long as it is privatized—as long as ecclesiastical institutions do not attempt to rally the faithful behind political proposals and as long as believers and unbelievers agree to follow a policy of live and let live" (33). For Rorty, the "epistemic arena" is a public space where parties negotiate about truth claims, space from which religion should retreat because it is not a discourse of negotiation (36). But the conditional features referred to by Rorty, who, by the way, was nonreligious but not antireligious, do not exist. Churches had a large role to play in getting millions of evangelicals to the polls in 2004, and unbelievers generally would be happy to sign a live-and-let-live deal long before believers do. Religion is not only an *always already* but perhaps an *always foreseeable* aspect of American public discourse. It is in this context that West asks, "For prophetic Christians like Martin Luther King Jr., his appeal to democratic ideals was grounded in his Christian convictions. Should he—or we—remain silent about these convictions when we argue for our political views?" (*Democracy Matters* 160).

West's concern with the prophetic extends to present international politics, especially affairs in the Middle East. In this thinking, a lasting peace will occur only when prophetic Jewish and Islamic voices, both here and abroad, gain persuasive ground. He notes that Islamic fundamentalism is sometimes a response to United States capitalism and imperialism, typified by the hedonistic behavior of ordinary American consumers and the turbocharged pursuit of oil by corporate interests. To West, Islamic clerics draw strength from these realities as well as from the support of the United States for oppressive regimes. West sees no future for American-style democracy in the Islamic world, but he does think that a more progressive medium can be reached between the influence and authority of clerics and democratic impulses like "voices of the demos, rotating elites, free expression of religion, culture, and politics, and uncoerced spaces for civic life" (*Democracy Matters* 138).

In any case, in a post–9/11 world, there is increased interest in discourses of the religious both in the public sphere and in protopublic classrooms of rhetorical education.[6] No deep reading and discussion of domestic or foreign policy fails to intersect with issues of religion at some point. West's prophetic voice, which highlights, echoes, and amplifies other prophetic voices, serves to illumine matters.

Race Matters Again

In 1990, educators Peter L. McClaren and Michael Dantley called for a critical pedagogy of race grounded solidly in the ideas of Cornel

West and Stuart Hall. An increase in the economic hardships faced by African Americans and the development of "emancipating strands" of knowledge, such as, critical theory, critical pedagogy, and cultural studies, signaled for McClaren and Dantley the exigency and opportunity to make teaching about race central to classrooms and to elevate the level of such instruction (30). But their intervention was not simply about African Americans. Race is a crucial dynamic in the structuring of all American subjectivities. Everyone, unless engaged in some serious reflection and action, assumes a historically determined role in the nation's racial-discourse hierarchy. As a discussant (unless, again, without some serious reflection and action), one will adopt a rhetorical default position concerning race and racism, which usually involves a highly emotional or intensely silent personal response. But because dispositions toward race and racism are not only personal but result partly from the materiality of discourse and because the most efficient antiracist activities are aided by the most critically informed stances on race and racism, examining "race matters," in West's lingo, or "languages of racism," in Hall's, is a vital component of a well-rounded rhetorical education.

For West, race represents the intersection wherein collide American imperial realities and democratic traditions. He notes in *Democracy Matters*, "The voices and viewpoints of reviled and disempowered Amerindians, Asians, Mexicans, Africans, and immigrant Europeans reveal and remind us of the profoundly racist roots of the first American empire—the old America of expansionist Manifest Destiny" (14). But in observing physical outcomes, West has never missed the link between discursive practices and racist oppression.

In *Prophesy Deliverance!* he highlighted the "way in which the very structure of modern discourse *at its inception* produced forms of rationality, scientificity, and objectivity as well as aesthetic and cultural ideals which require the constitution of the idea of white supremacy" (47) and stressed, "The initial structure of modern discourse in the West 'secretes' the idea of white supremacy" (48). As evidence, West cited the rise of positivism with its emphasis on observation and evidence and the huge influence of Rene Descartes, who speculated that scientific findings unerringly reflect the external world. In addition, he pointed to the classical revival, which began during the Early Renaissance and proceeded (though not in a linear fashion) to reach its peak in the middle of the eighteenth century. The classical revival was crucial to the development of white supremacist discourse because it privileged Greek aesthetic form. Greek physiognomy, then, constituted what West termed the "normative gaze" (53). The interplay of this normative gaze with positivism, mainly through the imperatives of natural historians, anthropologists, and phrenologists to measure and classify bodies, and rank races, formed the core of modern, white-supremacist discourse. The Greek image topped the rankings; the African was at the bottom. Therefore, West argued, the notion that Africans could be equal in beauty, culture, and intellect could not even exist within modernist epistemology (48). It is not unusual for contemporary critics to point to the racist views of influential Enlightenment figures like David Hume, Immanuel Kant, and, in the American grain, Thomas Jefferson, but West suggested that more noteworthy than the embrace of white supremacy by these thinkers is that they could embrace it *"without their having to put forward their own arguments to justify it"* (61; emphasis in the original). It is in this manner that modern discourse secreted the "major bowel" that is the idea of white supremacy (65).

West did not discount other explanations for the rise of racism, such as the logic of scholars like Rojer Sanjek and Theodore Allen, who, respectively, focus on the invention of "race" as a product of European global expansion that began in the fifteenth century and the ingenuous ploy of a slaveholding class in the American South to divide poor whites and enslaved Africans and thus secure power. West even offered alternate explanations. One focused on the biblical story of Ham and the curse of the black children. From other angles, in "Toward a Socialist Theory of Racism," he pointed to four conceptions of racism, ranging from a straight Marxist conception to one that conveys that there are racist states of mind that operate independently of a straight class analysis (97–99). West highlighted the discursive factor in *Prophesy Deliverance!* that is in that instance seen to be operative aside from concerns with class or the economy because he felt it had been theoretically underplayed, though it must be pointed out that complementary theories like Allen's also paid attention to discursive elements, the origin and popularity of "white" as an ethnic label, for example. However, the main point here is that all critical theories of race denaturalize racial schema, and to study the appearance and reification of these classification systems is to study how rhetorical formations, especially when entwined with institutional force, can promote white supremacy and stifle democracy. Or as West suggested in *Race Matters*, "How we set up terms for discussing racial issues shapes our perception and response to these issues" (3).

This last point also speaks to specific linguistic and literary dimensions of white supremacy that have been present in many classrooms of rhetorical education. Although every modern linguist embraces the doctrine of linguistic equality, the idea that no language variety is inherently superior or inferior to any other, students often still are judged—and judge—based on facility in Standardized English, the nation's institutional power tongue, which has a decidedly white tinge to it. Frequently, explicit assessments of intelligence, even character, correlate with the evaluated subject's performed distance from or proximity to the prestigious linguistic form. Implicitly, anyone whose language variety is not the privileged one in school is at a disadvantage. The disadvantage is not necessarily insurmountable, and there are reasons to gather the cultural capital of Standardized English. But it is a powerful message to send to students that the language they hold dear possesses no intellectual or epistemological gravity. Furthermore, to focus on a standard to be reached or reproduced while disregarding the different ways students may attempt to do so, especially when it is possible to build on the interests, talents, and strengths of students, is authoritarian, antidemocratic, and potentially disabling. Fortunately, there are useful forms and processes to draw on, "linguistic therapy" as Herbert Marcuse puts the matter in *An Essay on Liberation*, meaning the ability to "free words (and thereby concepts) from the all but total distortion of their meanings by the Establishment" (8). Thus "soul," Marcuse observes, a concept "lily-white ever since Plato," the "traditional seat of everything that is truly human," yet a "corny" and "false" term in dominant discourse (given historical presumptions about who can possess one), became a self-description of vitality and dynamism for African Americans (35–36). It became black truth.

This is not to say that "spoken soul," a coinage by Claude Brown and the title of an engrossing book by linguist John Rickford and his son, journalist Russell Rickford, is conceptually limiting. To the contrary, it is highly theoretical, usually with admirable and clarifying economy. For example, in rhetorical studies, we often speak of kairos or cite Lloyd Bitzer's famous discussion of the "rhetorical situation," which speaks to the need to recognize and respond to exigency as well as discusses the repercussions for failing to do so. Black folk wisdom sums up this understanding in five words: If you slow, you blow. Similarly, the aphorism "God helps those who help themselves" anticipates Vatz's much-discussed critique of Bitzer, that is, that one should create, not wait on exigency. But this proverb is not opposed to the earlier one. Black folk wisdom does not articulate a Bitzer-Vatz binary. It affirms, instead, that both taking opportunity *and* making opportunity are essential to progress.

Concerning literary matters, white supremacist logic, as McClaren and Dantley noted, motivate the maintenance of the exclusionary canon, what the authors called "Bloom's effete paradise" (37). Obviously, as West knows, the historical testimony that infuses sparkling examples of noncanonical literature represents a key democratic opportunity for schooling and for keeping a prophetic voice alive. As Victoria Earle Matthews spoke in 1895 about the "value of race literature" and the prospects that such writing would not be preserved, "Not only will the sturdy pioneers who paved the way and laid the foundations . . . be robbed of their just due, but an irretrievable wrong will be inflicted upon the generations that shall come after us" (147–48). Authoritarian culture warriors care little or nothing about Matthews's pronouncements, but democratic educators do.

There is no chance that *Race Matters*, if composition scholars have the say-so, will fall into obscurity anytime soon. It is by far West's most read and quoted publication in the field. Rather than attempt to catalogue the full response, I close this section with three examples, from Richard Marback, Krista Ratcliffe, and Morris Young, as representative.

In a helpful but flawed discussion, "Ebonics: Theorizing in Public Our Attitudes toward Literacy," Marback draws on West's discussion of nihilism and poverty in African America to establish a social and political background against which an informed dialogue about Ebonics could unfold.[7] He asserts, "West's claim to take seriously both the nihilistic threat of 'hopelessness, meaninglessness, and lovelessness' and the oppressive material conditions of inner city life is a strong counter to victim-blaming' (18). However, Marback, who offers no strong criticism of West, is savvy enough to include the perspective of Stephen Steinberg, who retorts that ruminations about the nihilism of African Americans accomplishes nothing in terms of practical solutions or change with respect to poverty and discrimination. In "The Liberal Retreat from Race during the Post–Civil Rights Era," Steinberg argues, "This nation's ruling elites need to be told that there is no exit from the current morass until they confront the legacy of slavery and resume the unfinished racial agenda. It is their nihilism that deserves condemnation—the crime, immorality, the self-destructive folly of tolerating racial ghettos and excluding yet another generation of black youth from the American dream" (40–41). It can hardly be denied that West actually has performed much of the telling to which Steinberg alludes. Yet, Steinberg's comment is noteworthy.[8] Eric Lott made similar remarks a few years earlier in a review of *Race Matters*, reading West as often portraying the black working class as passive and defeatist, almost helpless. Although Lott knows that West also speaks of black organizing and insurgency, he finds his use of the jungle metaphor to be an unfortunate description of the 'hood.[9] Lott views the black community to be more nuanced, activist, and always capable of exhibiting more agency than *Race Matters* conveys ("Cornel West" 43). He feels that the rhetorical task West set for himself, that is, to appeal to a broad, largely white, left-liberal audience or coalition, blocked him from appreciating or articulating the worth of race-based efforts or, as Lott phrases it, "black working-class self-activity" ("Cornel West" 43). Following the logic of C. L. R. James, Lott, who considers himself a comrade of West, contends that the black progressive bloc is a forceful political entity and, in matters of coalition building, should bring principled whites under its wing—not the reverse.[10]

Krista Ratcliffe, in "Rhetorical Listening: A Trope for Interpretive Invention and a 'Code of Cross-Cultural Conduct,'" reports on her attempts to problematize whiteness in her course. She applied "rhetorical listening" to her own language and that of others, a concept derived from her study of autoethnography, academic research, and personal stories. Ratcliffe explains her approach and its connection to West's book:

> My interest in listening to autoethnography initially emerged from a fascinating discussion that suddenly erupted a few years ago in my undergraduate rhetorical theory class. In response to Cornel West's *Race Matters*, an exasperated white student told the class, "I don't see what the big deal is. I don't wake up every morning, look in the mirror, and say, 'Hey, I'm a white man.'" I paused for a moment, letting the tension in the room build, and then I asked him, "Do you think that is West's point? That *you* don't have to think about race but *he* does?" What followed was the longest silence and then the most lively debate I have ever encountered in an undergraduate classroom, a debate about gender, race, and ethnicity that still echoes in my ears. (211)

Ratcliffe heard a variety of perspectives, including the "cultural voice of America that imagines itself racially unmarked" (211). She also encountered student expressions of frustration, tentativeness, defensiveness, and silence. She became conscious of her own teacherly, questioning tone. Seeing the value in opening up this space of inquiry in class, though being too hard on herself for not having done it sooner, Ratcliffe concludes, "Without this opportunity for listening, the young man and those who agreed with his ideas would never have been challenged, nor would have those students who whole-heartedly agreed with West, nor would have I" (212).

Near the close of *Minor Re/Visions: Asian American Literacy Narratives as a Rhetoric of Citizenship*, Young explains how West's work informs his own conceptualizing about the connections among race, language, discrimination, and literacy.

> Race matters in writing because, as I have argued, literacy and language have been used to discriminate against people of color but has also provided people of color with the means to respond to racism, to write their own stories and to write themselves into the American Story. Race matters in learning because it provides a framework to understanding how our experiences are different and similar, how our interactions in culture are generated and assessed. And race matters in teaching because what I do in the classroom is motivated by what I have experienced in my life. And my presence in the classroom will have an effect on the students who must interact with their Asian American teacher. (194–95)

Young is responding to West's remarks that race *matters* and that *race* matters involve "power and morality," "life and death" (*Race Matters* xi). In composition studies, we do not usually adopt quite as urgent a tone as West. But our work is bound up with matters of race, including the racialized nature of life chances and constriction.

Class Matters, Too

In her essay "Class Affects, Classroom Affectations," Julie Lindquist writes, "Paradoxically, in the professional literature on pedagogy within composition studies, class has been simultaneously everywhere and nowhere" (189). One of the reasons that class is hard to address as an analytic category in contemporary times is that the classic Marxist divisions among proletariat, middle class, and bourgeoisie do not obtain in a postindustrial, global economy (if they ever did). To be sure, clear distinctions can be made between the officially poor and the corporate elite, but it is harder to sort into class divisions all the social and economic gradations in between. The frugal blue-collar or service-working couple who owns a modest home outright and possesses a nest egg resembles in terms of economic status the middle class of, say, the Eisenhower 1950s more than does the overmortgaged, single-parent, white-collar manager or professional with no savings account suffering from serially maxed-out credit cards. The differences between our hypothetical blue-collar couple and beleaguered professional are likely to lie more in the realm of social mannerisms. But even if we posit a stable working class or middle class for argument's sake, these groups consist of bodies that are racialized and gendered—just to begin. One result is that on the American political landscape of recent decades, the drive for amelioration or social redress has been most forcefully or dramatically pursued along lines of race and gender. For example, racial and gender discrimination affect minorities and women of all economic classes, and a reformist measure like affirmative action has addressed that problem for minorities to a significant extent and, more significantly, for women. By contrast, such reformist interventions do little for the working or nonworking poor as a whole, among whose ranks are a disproportionate number of minorities and women, those who were not and will not be uplifted by race and gender legislation. Ironically, it was a great class movement, the labor movement of the Roosevelt era, which wrung concessions from industrialists while leaving antiracist and antisexist agendas woefully incomplete, that helped to set in motion both the modern American middle class and much of today's identity politics. This is not to argue against identity politics in general; progressive identity politics are indispensable. The important observation here is that identity politics on the whole, which run the gamut of perspectives regarding political economy, will have less-radical content than class-based initiatives. Moreover, the means of redress for the working class, namely, radical politics, does not appeal to many members of that group, many of whom are looking to escape it, aiming to improve their financial standing in a liberal, capitalist democracy and trying to shed indices of their origins along the way.

Most relevant for composition teachers is that they are often viewed by students as the examples of success, and their classrooms are seen as the vehicles of upward mobility. Sure, radical compositionists can lecture about how discourses of class are oppressive, but such talk is not perceived by students to be as related to their aspirations as insights about racism and sexism. The special issue on social class published by *College English* in 2004 signifies the strange status of class-based work in the field. Early in their essay "Struggling with Class in English Studies," Sherry Lee Linkon, Irvin Peckham, and Benjamin G. Lanier-Nabors acknowledge the functional weakness of class as a conceptual category: "We do not imagine class as an independent category of social relationships. Although it may be named and therefore provisionally isolated for the purpose of analysis and discussion, it should always be understood as intersecting with other categories of domination and oppression" (150). The same is true of other social categories, but the authors' quick theoretical caution seems to be less of a reflex for most race theorists or feminists. Jennifer Beech's "Redneck and Hillbilly Discourse in the Writing Classroom" also illumines the entanglement of class and race, for her piece is as much about one variable as the other. Nick Tingle, in "The Vexation of Class," provides an essentialist portrait of the working class as immobile, nontraveling, and nonperformative. He sees a fluid identity mostly to be the province of middle-class students (which it certainly is not, albeit the elements in play are different). Reflecting on his difficulties in college, Tingle suggests, "Perhaps things would have gone more smoothly if my middle-class college had taught the lessons of class, if there had been, for example, a course called 'The Working-Class Self.' But who knows whether I would have taken it, because I was so enraptured with high culture" (229). Readers may understand and even sympathize with Tingle's commentary, but few are likely to become overly emotional in response or accuse Tingle of selling out. But imagine—then consider class and composition further—if Tingle's story were about race, ethnicity, or gender and he recalled being so enamored with white or European or male culture that he might not have bothered with an available black studies, Latino studies, Asian American studies, Native American studies, or women's studies course.

In some ways, the most interesting developments around class in composition studies are the efforts to follow critical pedagogy to its logical extension and organize beyond the classroom. While it is fine to theorize about the emotional labor of being working class, respecting redneck commonplaces, or social ruptures, organizing is also tremendously valuable. It is in this vein that the ongoing project of Stephen Parks is heartening. He has been involved in a number of working-class, community-based literacy initiatives and has also written about class dynamics in composition studies. His book *Class Politics* is a signal document, not only as a history of the democratically inspired "Students' Right to Their Own Language" resolution adopted by CCCC in 1974 but as an example of how class matters intersect or, in some instances, collide with race matters.

Parks traced a history of the resolution that focused on the activism of white progressives like those in the New University Conference, who are seen to have pushed a progressive language policy on CCCC. In the process, Parks pilloried old-line ethnic models of activism and criticized the middle-class sensibilities of many African American professionals. He no doubt had a good point. But some of these same professionals excoriated Parks, not because they were called middle class but because they felt that Parks did not adequately represent the undeniably major contributions of African American academics to the language resolution, none of whom he bothered to interview. They had a good point as well. Fortunately, a major flare-up with back-and-forth arguments in professional journals, a prospect Parks feared, was avoided. For him the language-rights battle served as a metaphor for progressive struggle within CCCC, or as he phrased it, "The SRTOL was only my lever to produce a history highlighting the importance of collective action by academics" (5). Furthermore, Parks explained, "I hope to be heard as saying that class-based activism must always be integrated with actions to fight other forms of discrimination as well. I hope it is self-evident that I believe such activism must be a part of a faculty's career outside the classroom" (8). He feels that though perhaps there should be, there is no natural aligning of interracial forces fighting for social justice; thus, he has continued to reach out and attempt to forge alliances with other progressives, including African Americans, even while "straddling the line between naïve optimism about the ability of progressive caucuses to work together and pessimism about the current state of things" (253).

Recently, the delicate interplay of class and race—and I focus on this particular tandem because West has emphasized this linkage—was demonstrated to me unexpectedly when I shared with several black graduate students an article by Claude Hurlbert, Derek Owens, and Robert Yagelski that appeared in *Writing on the Edge*. The trio, who display left-liberal leanings at the least, criticized several aspects of the CCCC annual convention, including so-called run-of-the-mill panels and the "star system" of featured sessions. Owens, imagining that he had found some chink in CCCC's conservative armor, expressed unbridled wonder that his "subversive" proposal, with its nontraditional format, had been accepted for the 1999 CCCC convention in Atlanta. The fact of the matter is that I chaired that convention and was more than happy to have Owens present exactly in the manner that he did. Moreover, that session, on which Hurlbert appeared with him, was *not* in competition with any featured panel because I reduced the so-called star system for that convention. (This reflected my advocacy as a CCCC officer, though the tide of history has gone against me.) Owens in no way racialized his remarks. That the extended hand in Atlanta was a black one had no bearing on his criticism. But it did for my students. They were, like, "F them white boys." So touchy these students are.

In the long history of workers' struggle and antiracist activity in America, the energies of the two movements have combined with mixed results. White organizers of the radical kind, even socialist-democratic kind, within, say, CCCC, who would court, say, a black constituency, would do well, as would the intended constituency, to pay attention to the following observation by West.

> Black suspicion of white-dominated political movements (no matter how progressive) as well as the distance between these movements and the daily experiences of people of color have made it even more difficult to fight racism effectively. . . . Progressive organizations often find themselves going around in a vicious circle. Even when they have a great interest in antiracist struggle, they are unable to attract a critical mass of people of color because of their current predominantly white racial and cultural composition. These organizations are then stereotyped as lily white, and significant numbers of people of color refuse to join. ("Toward a Socialist Theory of Racism" 107)

The way beyond this impasse, as Parks knows, is through coalitions, though the tension between cultural or ethnic analyses, and class analyses is never easy to negotiate. Ultimately, West argues, *"Bonds of trust can be created only within concrete contexts of struggle"* ("Socialist Theory" 108; emphasis in the original). This is probably the first and best lesson for organizers.

Considering Foucault and the Prophetic

Cited even more widely than Cornel West in composition circles is the French philosopher, historian, and rhetorician Michel Foucault, whose writings have been influential for three primary reasons. First, his elaborate work to demonstrate the origin and development of a variety of discourses, his attention to the power relations embedded therein, and his explanation of the impact of discourses on the structuring of subjectivity line up well with composition's interest in social construction and critical pedagogy. Students cannot logically be asked, shown, or exhorted to resist oppressive and controlling discourses unless instructors can illustrate convincingly that those discursive formations, those much-discussed "regimes of truth," are indeed oppressive and exert undeniable influence on the students' sense of themselves even if students have been unaware of this. No one assists this pedagogical mission more than Foucault, who declared, in *The Order of Things*, "The fundamental codes of a culture—those governing its language, its schemas of perception, its exchanges, its techniques, its values, the hierarchy of its practices—establish for every man, from the very first, the empirical orders with which he will be dealing and within which he will be at home" (xx). It is in this spirit that Foucault offers the fruits of his archaeological and genealogical explorations that examine reigning knowledge complexes, or paradigms, and the statements they either discard or give rise to and infuse with meaning. In *The Archaeology of Knowledge*, Foucault uses as one example the statement, "The earth is round," whose substance is altered depending upon the context in which it is uttered. This statement, which to Foucault incorporates more than a literal sentence, cannot mean the same in pre-Copernicus and post-Copernicus eras because its relationship to other statements concerning the preposterousness or veracity of the claim is different in each instance (103). Semanticists possessed this insight before Foucault came along, but no linguist had applied this understanding across as wide a range of discursive activity as Foucault. Because of their focus on language as a historically manufactured object, his investigations inform specific concerns with authorship, textual interpretation, language diversity, and language policy. But this list is only preliminary. Scholars in composition are far from exhausting the applications of Foucault to their own projects.

Second, Foucault provides, at least on the one hand, clear political justification for radically inclined teachers of rhetorical education to pursue a radical agenda on the job. Because discourse is fundamental human behavior, it exists everywhere, including in the classroom. And because all discursive formations are laden with power, especially our civil, disciplining institutions, the classroom is a proper, even crucial venue in which to resist power. As Foucault suggests in *The History of Sexuality*, "Discourse transmits and produces power; it reinforces it, but also undermines and exposes it, renders it fragile and makes it possible to thwart it" (101). All power is to be resisted, according to Foucault; therefore, instructors can enact the role of his "specific intellectuals," countering pernicious effects of power in the local sites they inhabit professionally.[11] It is worthwhile work, but, on the other hand, a dilemma exists that turning to Foucault will not resolve. If power resides in all discourse, and all power is to be resisted, then students should be resisting their instructors, or, put another way, instructors should not be trying to teach in the first place because teaching is an exercise in power. This problem is transcended, of course, by acknowledging that different magnitudes of power circulate and being comfortable that your assault as an instructor on, say, culturally and institutionally sanctioned sexist discourse, is a lesser offense than, say, feminist or critical pedagogy. There is no way around judgment. Part of the reason Foucault flattens power is that he rejects analyses like Marxism that deal with power hierarchically and construct subjects strictly in terms of class relations. But this flattening is part of West's problem with Foucault's work, as will be evident shortly.

The third reason for Foucault's popularity in composition studies is that his function, as Paul Rabinow a quarter century ago predicted it would become, is that of a "founder of discursivity" among the post-1970s generation of academics. Foucault coined the term to describe figures like Karl Marx and Sigmund Freud, who wielded such rhetorical force that their writing organizes in substantial ways subsequent discourse. They still serve as major conceptual and methodological lenses, but their influence is not as great among younger scholars, disposed toward postmodernism and seeking less totalizing critiques of systemic power, as it was in earlier decades. Foucault's work, with its broad reach, and his celebrity status, which was no small factor, made him a prime candidate for adoption. In other words, from a perspective that he would appreciate, Foucault remains popular largely because at a certain postmodern moment, he was popularized.

Although West embraces Foucault's concern with the operation of powers and makes heavy use of the genealogical materialist mode of inquiry, he rejects what he calls Foucault's antiromanticism and the strong discourse move that focuses on subjects being constituted rather than "dynamic social practices" (*American Evasion of Philosophy*

225). Contrasting himself to Foucault, whom he feels severely under-theorized agency, he argues, "Human agency remains central—all we have in human societies and histories are structured and unstructured human social practices over time and space" (225). More important, West objects because Foucault "devalues moral discourse" and was overly reluctant to support mass political action (226). He applauds that "Foucault rightly wants to safeguard relentless criticism and healthy skepticism," yet he complains that "his rejection of even tentative aims and provisional ends results in existential rebellion or micropolitical revolt rather than concerted political praxis informed by moral vision and systemic (though flexible) analyses" (226). Cultural critics like West, on the other hand, "take seriously moral discourse—revisable means and ends of political action, the integrity and character of those engaged, and the precious ideals of participatory democracy and the flowering of the uniqueness of different human individualities" (226). West emphasizes that the prophetic-pragmatist critique of and resistance to "types of economic exploitation, state repression, and bureaucratic domination" are inextricably linked to "moral ideals of creative democracy and individuality" (226).

In a 1990 interview with Anders Stephanson, West and Stephanson discussed the worth of various critical conceptions, including the language models of Jürgen Habermas, Jacques Derrida, and Foucault.

> STEPHANSON: The earlier Foucaldian distinction between discursive and nondiscursive formations remains valid for you then?
>
> WEST: He should have held on to it, just as Habermas should have held on to his earlier notion of interaction—a notion rooted in the Marxist talk about social relations of production—rather than thinning it out into some impoverished idea of communication. Both can be seen as a move toward linguistic models for power.
>
> STEPHANSON: Even in the case of Foucault? His pan-power theories are, after all, discursive rather than purely *linguistic*.
>
> WEST: True. The later, genealogical Foucault would not make claims on linguistic models, but he remained more interested in power as it relates to the constitution of the subject than to power as such. Now, the structure of identity and subjectivity is important and has often been overlooked by the Marxist tradition; but forms of *subjection* and *subjugation* are ultimately quite different from "thick" forms of oppression like economic *exploitation*

or state *repression* or bureaucratic *domination*. At any rate, "the conditions for the possibility of the constitution of the subject" is a Kantian question to which there is no satisfactory answer. To answer it, as Heidegger said in his self-critique, is to extend the metaphysical impulse in the name of an attack on metaphysics. From that viewpoint, Foucault's notion of anonymous and autonomous discourses is but one in a series of attempts going back to Kant's transcendental subjects and Hegel's transindividual world spirits.

STEPHANSON: What if Foucault would have said that he recognized the existence of other types of oppression but that his field of analysis was simply different?

WEST: I would have replied, "Fine, but that sounds more like the language of an academic than a political intellectual." It would have been to fall into the same traps of disciplinary division of labor he was calling into question. If, in fact, one is writing texts that are strategic and tactical in relation to present struggles, then it is difficult to see how one can be counterhegemonic without actually including "thick" forms. (271–72)

Or as Mark David Wood surmises in his discussion of West, Marx, and Foucault, "The victims of racism, sexism, and exploitation would not get very far in their struggle to rid the world of these social ills on the basis of Foucault's concept of power" (61). Wood, favoring Marx and the Marxist leanings of West, as do I, believes that power is far less ambiguous and mobile than Foucault describes it, that is, as "at once visible and invisible, present and hidden, ubiquitous" (*Language, Counter-Memory, Practice* 213). Ruling classes do dominate through control of resources and state apparatuses. Back on the block, we know that we have some small-change ability to control phenomena, but we also figure that the big-finance dogs got *power's mammy*. It is only in a relatively minor sense that, as Foucault suggests, every individual can wield power (*Power/Knowledge* 72). It's not everybody who can authorize bombs *to* Iraq in some years or bombs *on* Iraq in others.

Some of my graduate students took umbrage at such criticism of Foucault, to them a founder, maybe even a hero, of discursivity. After reading *The American Evasion of Philosophy,* they said in effect, "West had better step stronger than this if he's going to take down Foucault." But the reality is that little exists in Foucault's oeuvre that can be used to cast West's claims as false. Foucault would defend himself against the charge that he undertheorized agency by noting that theorizing agency was a central concern of his: "I wanted not to exclude the problem of the subject, but to define the positions and functions that the subject could occupy in the diversity of discourse" (*Archaeology of Knowledge* 200).[12] But this simply is not the moralizing, prophetic social subject of West's imagination. West does overreach in his charge that Foucault had no ideal of freedom and held negative conceptions of critique and resistance (*American Evasion of Philosophy* 226). Foucault's vision is that one should be free of power and contest power everywhere. In this regard, Foucault would be in motion, just not volunteering for The Movement. His suspicion of mass action would remain. He stated unequivocally, in a concession to Marx, that "power is exercised the way it is in order to maintain capitalist exploitation" (*Language, Counter-Memory, Practice* 216). But Foucault, to West's dismay, would not struggle explicitly against such exploitation because that would mean the proletariat would lead him, which is a relationship he would not prefer. Instead, he would have everyone embrace a primary role in the struggle against power, which in his view implies that "they naturally enter as allies of the proletariat" (*Language, Counter-Memory, Practice* 216). Although a git-in-where-you-fit-in strategy does make some sense, for organizers this mystical formulation is only slightly less frustrating than his claim, however true, "I would say it's all against all. There aren't immediately given subjects of the struggle, one the proletariat, the other the bourgeoisie. Who fights against whom? We all fight each other. And there is always within each of us something that fights something else" (*Power/Knowledge* 208).

In the end, it is not a matter, I would have my students know, of arbitrating between West and Foucault (though they gotta tighten up they game if they gon take down West). You appropriate from each what you can use. Foucault's insights are valuable, and he would not be against prophetic witness. Of course, he would primarily be interested in such discourse in terms of how it functions as a way to talk about power. Paul Rabinow captured it simply concerning Foucault: "He is not an intellectual prophet" (23). Yet, Foucault enables West's methodology, though not his radically prophetic impulses.

5
Tragicomic Hope in Democracy

CORNEL WEST defines the tragicomic as "the ability to laugh and retain a sense of life's joy—to preserve hope even while staring in the face of hate and hypocrisy—as against falling into the nihilism of paralyzing despair" (*Democracy Matters* 16). In an American context, this psychic technique is anchored to a blues sensibility and blues vision that afford a clear and unflinching gaze at our nation's historical failures. For West, this psychological posture is fundamental, not transient, and is a stance from which he habitually engages society. As George Yancy notes, "Not only is West a blues man in the world of ideas, but he also adopts, through his emphasis on affirming life in the midst of tragedy, a blues ontology, a mode of being which is affirmative in the face of existential and social adversity" (8). Crucial to this experiment in living are the inspiring notes and chords of African American music, that brilliant joyful noise and pain-tinged expression of black humanity. Such cultural outpouring, as Rosemary Cowan points out and West knows, "performs a vital preservative function by helping to maintain human vitality of life in the face of storms of oppression, and by emphasizing creativity and dignity rather than self-pity" (26). Tragicomic hope, therefore, as a discursive strategy derived from a basic spiritual-blues framework necessarily evokes the indomitable, keep-on-pushing sensibility reflected in the high plateaus of African American music and its organic connection to the black freedom struggle.[1] On the track "The Journey," from his 2001 CD, *Sketches of My Culture*, West pays tribute to this music, hailing, in sequence, the achievements of the spirituals, the blues, jazz, soul, and hip-hop. In this chapter, I link a relatively late development on this tragicomic continuum, namely, a strand of the sublime 1960s and early 1970s soul and funk of my youth, back to one of its lyrical wellsprings, the spirituals, and then forward to an energetic, occasionally brilliant, and sometimes wayward offspring in need of the guidance of tradition, hip-hop. I then aim to indicate the relevance of this exploration to current pedagogical efforts related to critical-language awareness.

Poets of Soul

Among the numerous soul artists one could have mentioned on a track like "The Journey," West selected Aretha Franklin, Luther Vandross, Marvin Gaye, and Curtis Mayfield. Vandross is a decade or so younger than the other three and, in any event, never reached any phase of the socially conscious song making that concerns me here. Mayfield, on the other hand, with tunes like "Keep on Pushing," "People Get Ready," which was also recorded by Franklin, and "We're a Winner," combined with Franklin ("Respect"), Sam Cooke ("A Change Is Gonna Come," another song Franklin covered), James Brown ("Say It Loud, I'm Black and I'm Proud"), and Gaye ("What's Going On," "Mercy, Mercy Me," and "Inner City Blues") to provide the key highlights of the soundtrack of the modern Civil Rights Movement and, to some extent, the Black Power/Black Arts era. Mayfield, in particular, stands out as the prototypical writer and performer who articulated 1960s and 1970s black pain, struggle, and aspirations.

I am not arguing that attending to political struggle was all consuming for Mayfield. When the 1960s began, he was seventeen years old. He had other business to handle. He had to talk about pure enchantment with women, as in "Gypsy Woman" (1961) and the hormonally attuned "Never Let Me Go" (1962). You know the spiel, something along the lines of, "Love me right now, tonight. Gotta be tonight, can't wait." Mayfield was popping high-tenor game to the coy and not-so-coy mistresses. He was a soulful version of an Andrew Marvell persona, making the sun run while the Impressions backed him up in neo–doo wop. Then, of course, came the recordings vowing unreserved love. Sterling examples are "I'm the One Who Loves You" (1963) and the truly masterful "I'm So Proud" (1964). Then came the adamant denial of any cheating: "You Must Believe Me" (1964). You know, he just happened to be at the party with that other woman. That's all it could be. Him cheat? Impossible. Then the recording about indeed cheating and being sorry about it and seeking forgiveness, if the girlfriend can only find it in her heart to begin anew. This is "See the Real Me'" (1964). We even heard a rendition of what might be called one of the payback chronicles, the indignant "*You've Been Cheatin'*" (1965; emphasis added). I don't claim the songs are autobiographical—although crooning falsetto voices can find a lot of trouble—only that Mayfield had plenty of fun and success with various aspects of African American life, some of which has its airy and comic dimensions, as you know, along with its blue moods.

At an expressly social level, however, young Mayfield, repulsed by the monumental racism and inequality in America, also became a poet of the black oppressed. He provided an important voicing in the striving for integration, which was the dominant strand of African American political activity, with the emblematic figure being Martin Luther King Jr. Indeed, Mayfield's 1964 hit "Keep On Pushing" reflects the optimism of the recently concluded March on Washington for Jobs and Freedom. A people full of soul, that black, animating impulse hard to define but easy to recognize, will struggle inexorably toward success on the racial front. To paraphrase the songwriter, these people have their strength, and therefore it doesn't make any sense not to keep on pushing—keep pushing the stone walls to the side with their determination and pride, pushing, despite setbacks like the assassination of Medgar Evers, on to the Civil Rights Act of 1964 and the Voting Rights Act of 1965. Mayfield would use the refrain "keep on pushing" on several more recordings, including "Amen" (1965) and "Meeting Over Yonder" (1965), both examples of his prophetic witness and his attempt to call the African American masses to activism in the socioreligious language they best understood. Mayfield's most famous call in this vein is "People Get Ready" (1965), and for this political performance, he turns to the spirituals, that reservoir of six thousand or so songs that assert brilliantly the humanity and perseverance of an enslaved population laboring within the brutal American slavocracy. Those black and unknown bards, as James Weldon Johnson referred to them, blended African discourse, such as, culturally specific epics and praise poems, with the King James Bible, yielding a host of verses that spoke of freedom, though in a muted or coded manner.

Of course, I am embracing a political interpretation of the spirituals even as I acknowledge a long-running controversy about their true import. Some view them as the simple and plaintive yearnings of a servile people looking toward heaven for salvation. The enslaved, in this view, could emote pain and longing but not develop a whole system of coded messages. But although heaven might have represented the ultimate salvation, many folks were getting their earthly move and groove on. At the height of American enslavement, there were fifty thousand escape attempts annually, about one thousand per week. Songs like "Steal Away to Jesus" were integral to the collective effort:

> Steal away, steal away, steal away to Jesus,
> Steal away, steal away home,
> I ain't got long to stay here.
>
> My Lord, He calls me,
> He calls me by the thunder,
> The trumpet sounds within-a my soul,
> I ain't got long to stay here.

A lot of people heard the thunder sound within their souls (a prearranged sound signal to get in motion) and then stole away to Jesus (who welcomed folks up North). At this juncture, one has to be willfully ignorant to miss all of the movement in the spirituals. Sweet chariots swinging low, boats to sail, the Gospel Train a-coming. And after reading *Hidden in Plain View*, Jacqueline L. Tobin and Raymond G. Dobard's book on the secret messages sewn into quilts, one should certainly be suspicious of claims that the enslaved lacked semiotic sophistication and were only singing about a soul's passage to heaven.

Had the enslaved been aware of someone like, say, Mikhail Bakhtin, they would have appreciated him. They knew about heteroglossia and certainly were aware that on a basic semantic level, different languages were being spoken around them, for they fundamentally were speaking the language of freedom and were being addressed by masters and representatives of the masters in the language of enslavement. They understood the master's centrifugal official feast and the need for their own centripetal carnival. But because of their limited mobility, they also knew that the carnival and the official feast had to merge for them spatially. *They had to be at they own carnival at the same time that they was all up inside the official feast.*[2] They were the preacher in Paul Laurence Dunbar's compellingly wrought "Ante-Bellum Sermon." In the poem, what the preacher is saying about Moses and liberation is simply about the Scriptures—if you are not the right audience.

> *An' de lan' shall hyeah his thundah,*
>   *Lak a blas' f'om Gab'el's ho'n,*
> *Fu' de Lawd of hosts is mighty*
>   *When he girds his armor on.*
> *But fu' feah some one mistakes me,*
>   *I will pause right hyeah to say,*
> *Dat I'm still a-preachin' ancient*
>   *I ain't talkin' 'bout to-day.*

(45)

But if you are the right audience, then impending liberation is the subject.

> *But I tell you, fellah christens,*
>   *Thing's happen mighty strange;*
> *Now, de lawd done dis fu' Isrul,*
>   *An' his ways don't nevah change.*

(45)

In the final stanza, the preacher "slips" by inserting a first-person pronoun.

> *But when Moses wif his powah*
>   *Comes an' sets us chillun free*

(46)

Yet the message remains sufficiently obscure—and clear—for all concerned.

Although not every spiritual is overtly political (a compromise somewhere between none and all that I accept), it is precisely the arguably political ones that have been of most interest to African American writers and artists. That is why it was predictable that in 1965, the twenty-two-year-old Mayfield would urge the people to get ready because there's a train a-coming, scooping up those passengers, those freedom fighters, from coast to coast. This is the childhood Chicago peer of Emmett Till, who was murdered in Mississippi by white racists for allegedly whistling at a white woman. This is the church-raised observer of Montgomery, Little Rock, and the festivities in Washington but also of Birmingham, or "Bombingham." Mayfield was morphing into full adulthood and pleading with African Americans and the general populace to get on board because the issues of justice and equality had yet to be decided, legislative gains notwithstanding. They *will* be decided in favor of the dispossessed and not the bigots and evil profiteers, or so the song proclaims, though more solemnly than on earlier tracks, because God sides with the oppressed, and there is no hiding place against the kingdom's throne. Thus, Mayfield samples lyrics from a travel spiritual like the "The Gospel Train."

> She's nearing now the station
> O, sinner, don't be vain
> But come and get your ticket
> And be ready for the train.

He merges the import of these lines with the rallying cry about God's inevitable triumph expressed in the spiritual "There's No Hiding Place Down There."

> O, I went to the rock to hide my face
> The rock cried out, "No hiding place"
> There's no hiding place down there.

As Mayfield consulted the spirituals for content, the double-voiced nature of some of the songs also worked for him. We heard the political message. Craig Werner, for example, points out that some activists modified lyrics to proclaim, "There's no hiding place when the Movement comes" and "Everybody wants freedom, this I know" (125).[3] But we also could deny that there was a political message in "People Get Ready." Black-oriented radio, therefore, not necessarily a paragon of progressivism, despite the presence of some hip disc jockeys, could proceed relatively undisturbed. Things changed, however, in 1967, with the release of "We're a Winner," an overtly bolder statement than Mayfield's previous ones, asserting that folks should follow the advice of their political leaders. The semantic item *leaders*, mainly meaning King, who was more of a radical at that point than he had been in 1963, undercuts the possibility of double entendre. This song is thus an explicit endorsement of black political activism, even a statement of defiance and a gesture to Black Powerists with the suggestion that African American activists would henceforth be tearless and fearless.

The songwriter reflected the don't-mind-dying challenge of an earlier generation of urban bluesmen.

For this song, Mayfield did catch some flak from black-oriented radio stations, pressured by the right, that were reluctant to play the record. As Mayfield himself remarked, "When you're talking about songs such as 'We're a Winner,' that's locked in with Martin Luther King. Just its existence could cause some controversy. But it was a song with a message; it had an inspiring message. And this wasn't really what radio was about in those times" (Pruter 7). For the most part, the same is true today. Nonetheless, Mayfield forwarded a similarly inspiring message in "We're Rolling On" (1968), advising that efforts for social justice won't stop until the proverbial mountaintop has been reached. This song was recorded on March 15, less than three weeks before King's "mountaintop speech," and it is interesting to note the parallel between the two utterances and the continual use of vertical mobility in Mayfield's lyrics. As Keith D. Miller informs us, a rich metaphorical network both saturates and underlies African American expressive culture (547). *Up* and *mountaintop* are two of the primary metaphorical elements in this structure, paramount terministic screens in the Burkean sense, so "moving up" and "reaching mountaintops" are not simply creative or colorful descriptions, they function as intense psychic bonding (547–48). Both King and Mayfield knew this when they tapped into this metaphorical network—King to reach his audience face-to-face and Mayfield in a bid for airplay.

In some respects, the most intriguing song that Mayfield recorded in the 1960s is "Fool for You" (1968), one of his first efforts after King's assassination and one reflective of diminished optimism, even bitterness. On the surface, a ballad about a man stuck hopelessly on a woman who never does the singer's persona right, the song, however, contains no explicit references to a female body. Perhaps America is the woman. If Mayfield experienced difficulty securing airtime for the celebratory "We're a Winner," then he had to know that a bitter critique of the nation, despite his being rooted incontrovertibly and lovingly in it, could pose a problem. So is it farfetched to assume that Mayfield visited the spirituals yet again, not simply for content but to evoke the double-voiced rhetorical strategy? Consider, for example, that the same recording period yielded other political statements, all milder—slightly milder in "This Is My Country" (1968), which includes testimony about three hundred years of suffering, and much more mildly so in "Choice of Colors" (1969), which proclaims education as the key and evokes the signature anthem of civil rights demonstrators, namely, "We Shall Overcome." Where, then, was the immediate post-King rage? I contend that waiting for radio to loosen up a bit more, that rage is encapsulated in the devastatingly poignant "Fool for You."

As Mayfield entered the 1970s, nearly a legend at the age of twenty-seven, he continued to spin out hits, keep-on-pushing entries like "Move on Up" (1970) and tender, old-school ballads like "The Makings of You" (1970), "So in Love" (1975), and "Only You, Babe" (1976). He also, in a somewhat freer radio atmosphere, expressed strident social and political commentary in songs like "If There's a Hell Below We're All Going to Go" (1970), which is largely a critique of the Nixon administration. More important, he remained an exemplar of the tragicomic, believing in the good that many people possess and continually trying as an artist, despite the day's hardships, which would eventually include his own physical paralysis, to forge a connection with that good.

If Mayfield was the soul artist who most consistently embraced the Civil Rights Movement, Aretha Franklin was the most resounding soul voice. "Respect," her 1967 mega hit that topped both the R&B and pop charts, served as a pulsating anthem for the dispossessed. Literally about a woman demanding the props that she deserves from her man, especially since she's in the process of forking over all of her money, which is a fortune not to be trifled with, the song has been hailed as both a feminist and racial proclamation, even as a specifically integrationist rallying cry given the white musicians who make up the stirring horn section. As engineer Tom Dowd remarked, "It could be a racial situation, it could be a political situation, it could be just the man-woman situation" (qtd. in Bego, *Queen of Soul* 88). Producer Jerry Wexler, less inclined to promote the racial angle, nonetheless asserted that the song represents "a very interesting mix: an intuitive feminist outcry, a sexual statement, and an announcement of dignity. And a minority person making a statement of pride without sloganeering" (qtd. in Bego, *Queen of Soul* 89). But as an African American singer, Aretha Franklin did not have to sloganeer. The term *respect*, like *up* and *mountaintop*, is a centerpiece of the black metaphorical network and is therefore always already an amplified racial declaration. Moreover, given continual black suffering, few items in the African American lexicon are more salient than *respect*, which is why the term passes from generation to generation with such force and why its real or perceived negation, *disrespect* or *diss*, constitutes, for better or worse, such an egregious affront in the black community.

No astute critic, then, reads this blazing remake of Otis Redding's 1965 entry to be about a single instance of female-male negotiation. It may be about female-male interaction writ large but also, as Matt Dobkin asserts, "For other listeners who felt the racial implications of the song more forcefully than its feminist-sexual undercurrents, 'Respect' was the sound of revolution" (7). This is not to argue that Franklin explicitly embraced the politics of Black Power. The singer termed her song "one of the battle cries of the civil rights movement" (Franklin and Ritz 112). She was a dyed-in-the-wool King supporter who performed numerous benefits for the Southern Christian Leadership Conference. Early in 1968, on Aretha Franklin Day in Detroit, King flew into the city to present her with a service award from the organization. But Franklin did not need to advocate Black Power in the fashion of Stokely Carmichael to tap into the Black Power mood. As Werner observes, "Even many who weren't impressed with Black Power's ideology responded favorably to the emotional punch of slogans like 'Black Is Beautiful' and 'Power to the People.' 'R-E-S-P-E-C-T' spelled the same thing to them, without the ideological baggage and with a gospel call to freedom on the backbeat" (134).

Of course, the cultural significance of an artifact like "Respect" does not rely solely on intrinsic textual qualities. Because of the power of metaphor and the mental capacities of readers, a text can accrue any number of meanings. In that regard, a song by Mayfield or Franklin or one of the spirituals is not unique. I have indicated the double-voiced quality of certain lyrics to acknowledge the composing complexity (often denied) of the creators, just as literary scholars give proper due when they perceive that an author's intention or reception is multilayered. Yet, a text, made public, must function in the social universe, and this involves processes of interpretation. One form of interpretation known as cultural criticism dictates, according to Mary Poovey, that culture be studied as "an interdependent set of institutional and informal practices and discourses" and explores "the traces this larger social formation produces in individual texts" (620). The object of focus, therefore, is not "just the individual text, but something extrapolated from a wide variety of texts and reconstructed as the ideological and material conditions of possibility *for* these texts" (622). In other words, why not covert messages on the plantation when overt expression was subject to punishment? And why not drape Black Power meaning on a text in the wake of the Watts uprising of 1965, the flames of Hough in 1966, and King's ineffective organizing foray into Chicago that same year? So the ultimate point is not that "Respect" *could* be read as a revolutionary race anthem, especially by large numbers of black urban youth, a group I then belonged to, but that it *was*.

Poovey's view of cultural criticism suggests a method of teaching literature and writing courses that she, after Cornel West, calls "de-disciplinary" (623).[4] She cites West's "Minority Discourse and the Pitfalls of Canon Formation" to indicate how fostering the critical abilities of contemporary students should involve grappling with cultural output beyond that of the traditional literary canon. The spirituals, Mayfield, and Franklin are thus, for West, reasonable places to start. Poovey herself possesses understandably strong leanings toward the music of Bruce Springsteen, though of course, as Werner reminds us, she should note Mayfield's strong influence on Springsteen, especially on *The Rising*, what Werner calls Springsteen's "blue-eyed gospel masterpiece" (*Higher Ground* 290).

"Respect," though the greatest, was not the only black political anthem that Franklin offered in the 1960s. "Think" (1968) is also ostensibly about a couple's interaction but clearly speaks to larger concerns. The bridge contains fifteen words, twelve of which are the word *freedom*, which is belted out exuberantly. It is not a particularly sensual song as Franklin songs go. It is not "Natural Woman" or "Dr. Feelgood," for example. Instead, it fed into an evolving militant mood, in some ways with more urgency and edginess than "Respect." "Ain't No Way" (1968) operates more calmly, suggesting a quietly reflective pose relative to the impasse of the Civil Rights Movement. Enduring racism has stalled the advance of the love ethic, and love is strictly conditional in this formulation. The subject cannot do it if the object will not permit it. A similar but more pleading song, which is also a physical one in the manner of Mayfield's "Fool for You" and thus easily read as social complaint, is "Share Your Love with Me" (1969). Though somewhat somber, a tone at odds with its title, the song calls for harmony and peace, and it stresses the possibility of connection and expresses an optimism that is not blind but is sorrowfully insightful.

Franklin essentially, like Mayfield, is a paragon of the keep-on-pushing, people-get-ready sensibility derived from the spiritual-blues impulse. She does one album all in blue—*Delta Meets Detroit*

(1998)—on which she sings blues classics like "Going Down Slow" and "The Thrill Is Gone." On the latter song, she bends genre and includes a chorus, sung by background singers Margaret Branch, Brenda Bryant, and Almeda Lattimore, which samples the same spiritual that King did most famously. They sing, "Thank God Almighty, free at last." Franklin uses all the black musical resources at her disposal as she suggests the spectacular things to be achieved by all those spirits in the dark.

Although three years older than both Mayfield and Franklin, Marvin Gaye remained mostly on the political sidelines throughout the 1960s, more of a checkbook activist than an artistic commentator. He felt no less indignant or radical. He once commented on his upbringing in segregated Washington, D.C., "How's the average black kid supposed to buy the Bill of Rights when he sees on the street that his own rights aren't worth shit?" (Ritz 34). Gaye admired Malcolm X and appreciated his "strength and truth-telling" and also respected what he called King's "idealism and courage" (106). However, a lack of resolve on Gaye's part and Motown's emphasis on spinning out music that Berry Gordy felt would be palatable to a crossover audience rendered him publicly silent at the height of the Civil Rights and Black Power Movements. One could have asked him, "Ain't that peculiar?" But although Gaye arrived late to the party, he took it over with one fell swoop, the 1971 release of *What's Going On*, an album considered by many, including Cornel West, to be, in West's words, "the greatest album in Afro-American popular music" ("In Memory of Marvin Gaye" 175). A haunting meditation on pressing social ills, Gaye, in the estimation of Michael Eric Dyson, "made it clear that social justice is what love sounds like when it speaks in public" (72).

Prompted by opening background vocals asking him what's happening, Gaye provides a remarkably creative and expansive response in the spiritual-blues impulse, with no need for subtlety or subterfuge. The lead and title track protests against the war in Vietnam, with Gaye admonishing the power structure not to punish brutally those with the conscience and nerve to engage in antiwar demonstrations. In "What's Happening Brother," we get a portrait of the bleak, urban, no-work, no-job reality facing many African American Vietnam veterans, his brother Frankie Gay in particular. "Flyin' High," a forerunner to Stevie Wonder's "Too High," addresses the drug infestation in urban communities. The most urgent and impassioned plea on the album is Gaye's call on "Save the Children." Sadly, he expresses a sentiment no less true or less urgent today than thirty-seven years ago. Gaye mines his Christian faith and the depth of the love ethic in "God Is Love," and he presses this perspective in "Right On" and "Wholy Holy."

Of the two other hit singles on the album, aside from the title tune, "Mercy Mercy Me" protests the corporate and government devastation of the environment signaled by air pollution, oil spills in the ocean, and radioactive waste. "Inner City Blues" rails against the prioritizing of space exploration over the reduction of poverty, high taxes, inflation, unmanageable bills, the war, and police brutality, all of which had especially debilitating effects on inner cities. Both of these songs were covered almost immediately in fabulous fashion by standout saxophonist Grover Washington Jr., which was testimony to their resonance. *What's Going On* was the zenith of Gaye's artistic achievement and perhaps of his tortured life, as he thereafter succumbed to family dysfunction and to the drug plight he illumined so well. One of the most tragic figures in the soul tradition, he soared high, though, before his death at the hands of his father.

In Search of Prophetic Hip-Hop

Among the things that connect soul artists to the hip-hop generation are thematic explorations of the tragic by the soul artists and some of their early 1970s work as part of the revolution in funk. Mayfield best symbolizes this lyrical and rhythmic link through his album *Superfly*, the 1972 soundtrack for the blaxploitation flick of the same name. Rather than churning out the usual, mostly instrumental soundtrack, Mayfield wrote lyrical portraits of some of the main characters. So on "Pusherman," we hear about the mean Ghetto Prince, a man with the hottest women who is also a capable supplier of cocaine and marijuana. Many young hip-hoppers love this character portrayal. So do I, as I am tolerant of a neobadman some days. But operating contrapuntally, Mayfield includes cautionary tales on the album. Freddie, after all, is dead. The drug dealer Eddie, succumbing to greed and a lack of social awareness, is probably not going to survive either. And the lively antidrug, natural-high anthem "No Thing on Me (Cocaine Song)" is intended as the ideologically dominant track, notwithstanding the emphases of the film itself.[5] The Superfly persona is real, as in kept real, but is not ultimately admirable or transcendent—which it should not be.

One way to phrase the challenge of contemporary African American rap music, one it has met with mixed results, is that it needs to achieve the balance of Mayfield's album. It must articulate a Superfly ethos, which is a nonextractable tragic element of the social matrix from which rap music stems and simultaneously expresses, and, if it is to be true to the legacy of the spiritual-blues impulse, an unambiguous and somewhat upbeat message in support of radical democratic ideas. Or as West, in the essay "On Afro-American Popular Music: From Bebop to Rap," referring specifically to black rap, phrased it, "The vitality and vigor of Afro-American popular music depends not only on the talents of Afro-American musicians, but also on the moral visions, social analyses, and political strategies which highlight personal dignity, provide political promise, and give existential hope to the underclass and poor working class in Afro-America" (187). Or as he put the matter more recently in *Democracy Matters*, "The best of rap music and hip-hop culture still expresses stronger and more clearly than any cultural expression in the past generation a profound indictment of the moral decadence of our dominant society" (179). Distinguishing the prophetic brand of rap music from a hedonist, hyperviolent, misogynist variety that has proven commercially viable, a form he labels Constantinian, he follows, "Prophetic hip-hop has told painful truths about their internal struggles and how the decrepit schools, inadequate health care, unemployment, and drug markets of the urban centers of the American empire have wounded their souls. . . . Prophetic hip-hop is precious soil in which the seeds of democratic individuality, community, and society can sprout" (183–85). Yet, as to be expected, West has not been overly optimistic about the possibilities. In 1989, when asked where rap music would end up, he replied, "Where most American postmodern products end up: highly packaged, regulated, distributed, circulated, and consumed" (Stephanson 281).

Unfortunately, West's prediction almost two decades ago has been largely accurate, yet the battle for the soul of hip-hop, as Manning Marable and Craig S. Watkins would put the matter, continues. In "The Politics of Hip Hop," Marable states, "There has always been a struggle for the 'soul' of hip hop culture, represented by the deep tension between politically-conscious and 'positivity' rap artists versus the powerful and reactionary impulses toward misogyny, homophobia, corporate greed, and crude commodification" (2). Watkins, in *Hip Hop Matters*, a marvelously insightful account about the rise and state of hip-hop culture and its pervasive impact on the broader world, including the academic sphere, ultimately extends the hope that prophetic hip-hop will emerge as the centerpiece of a progressive political movement. He wishes that lyrical high points reminiscent of the best of Chuck D, Queen Latifah, Melle Mel, and KRS-One, would prevail in the public sphere over hyperviolent, misogynist, corporate hip-hop and help to galvanize mass action toward social justice. Indeed, those voices represent artistic peaks: Queen Latifah's searing cry of UNITY and sage advice for us, young African American women in particular, as well as her succinct analyses of the evil that men do; Melle Mel's magisterial verse on the stellar "The Message," shedding light on realities based in inner-city blight; KRS-One, the T'Cha, positing positive values in the face of "problemz" of corporate greed and structural racism, ever attuned to the question in the rap game of prophets versus profits; and Chuck D bringing the noise, eternal optimism, and stinging critiques of mainstream media, though Flav has done his best to tarnish the legacy with his adventures in so-called reality television, the kind of trash he trashed in "She Watch Channel Zero?!"

Can wonderful postmodern moments be repeated and amplified like the one in February 2003 when Chuck D took to the Carnegie Hall stage with blues legend John Lee Hooker and literally rooted hip-hop in the spiritual-blues impulse by flippin the script and chanting the antiwar sentiment "No Boom Boom Boom" as Hooker accompanied him on guitar by playing "Boom Boom Boom Boom," his classic song that is as far removed in its concern from an invasion of Iraq as a song can get? Can a "ghetto anthem" similar to Jay-Z's 1998 "Hard Knock Life" spur amelioration of the plight of the poor? ("Hard Knock Life" was so commercially successful that when ABC broadcast its 1999 version of *Annie*, the network chose to feature in its trailers "It's a Hard Knock Life" over "Tomorrow," which had long been the show's signature song, a decision that was directly and solely responsible for the fact that this then-forty-something viewer tuned in to the show.) Or will the preponderance of popular lyrics, including much of the post-hard-knock corpus of Jay-Z, not even suggest that political direction?

Of course, a debate rages over whether specific expectations should be an issue—which make them an issue. A quick Google search with the terms *socially conscious hip-hop* and *politically conscious hip-hop* reveals dozens of Web pages and listservs on which the controversy is discussed. Added to the mix is contention about whether any artist should be called upon to lead political initiatives and whether one even could. Additional verbal sparring unfolds over whether the true import of rap's origins lies in consciously political critique or the single-minded drive to rock the party. Such exchanges splinter quickly into binaries but generally lead to a reasonable consensus or at least a truce. The tentative truths are that rap as a whole has always embraced both politics and parties; political commentary is not a necessary feature of the music but certainly can be an important one. Activism, raptivism in this instance, can be helpful but needs to align with other forces. The overall discussion parallels very closely debates about the socially responsible writer that have been a key feature of literary conferences for decades. I was seated on a panel next to Amiri Baraka a few years ago at one of those conferences. A young woman from the audience, after hearing Baraka expound about the social responsibility of writers, responded that she knew what her responsibility would be in the morning but sometimes just wanted to read about someone shaking her booty in the club at night. Anyone on the hip-hop trail is familiar with this polemic.

Yet, a long list of rappers, ones that West would cast in the prophetic vein, remains warm to the task of generating politically conscious hip-hop. The artist Common, for example, on his CD *Be* (2005), manages to merge descriptions of Southside Chicago with tributes to figures like John Coltrane, Malcolm X, and the Last Poets. The Last Poets, a group I first spotted on Ellis Haizlip's *Soul* back in the day and who are sometimes considered the "fathers of spoken word," perform on the track "The Corner." They contribute commentary about the positive site the corner was in their youth as contrasted to Common's portrayal of the current situation. Of course, the Last Poets are putting an idyllic, revisionist spin on matters. Some corners in the 'hood were indeed positive spaces, but the generic category "corner" (and I was on many) was hardly an unproblematic sanctuary of progressive thought and action. Nonetheless, the cut does inspire, as does "Love Is" and "It's Your World."

Although Common illumines well the present, he does not project a prophetic sense, in terms of suggesting concrete possibilities, as strongly as Talib Kweli. (But all of my remarks about Kweli are overly biased because I first met him when he was about ten years old.) A dazzling lyricist—no one flows better day in and day out—Kweli's corpus is both critical and visionary. He limns street realities but is not limited by them. And he displays literary knowledge beyond what you ordinarily hear on popular recordings. Where else in rap or any music do you get references to W. E. B. Du Bois, as is the case on "Gun Music" (2002), or to Norman Mailer, on "Get By" (2002), to James

Joyce, on "Memories Live" (2000), or to Octavia Butler and to Haki Madhubuti's Third World Press, on "Ms. Hill" (2005). I wonder about the peaceful Du Bois when I listen to "Gun Music," but Du Bois did guard his home with a shotgun during the Atlanta race riot in 1906.

Important dimensions of Kweli's humanity are displayed on tracks like "Joy" (2002), his heartfelt and heart-warming expression—with Mos Def spurring him on—of love and pride upon the birth of his children. Not enough children are welcomed into the world with this amount of affection. Kweli's prophetic side is manifest on "Africa Dream" (2000). "Ms. Hill" is a blues reaching out to Lauryn Hill, once the brightest of hip-hop stars. We all should hope that she resurges with her artistic proposals to direct government power to a focus on alleviating American poverty. Could Hill or Kweli push it more?

M-1 and Stic.Man, who make up the duo Dead Prez (bang on out, fellas!), are two of the very few avowed socialist rappers in the game. They adopt the stance without naïvete. Their "Animal in Man" (2000) is a parody of Orwell's *Animal Farm*, with some of the same conclusions about dispositions toward totalitarianism by the formerly oppressed. Nonetheless, they see their work as a cultural weapon, however humble, against capitalism, imperialism, and white supremacy. In an interview aired during the Dead Prez television special in 2006, Stic.Man, characterizing the nation's business operations as neoslavery, assessed, "The plantation, it's in McDonald's. It's in Sony. It's in Virgin. It's the American system of exploitation. You work for me for crumbs while I build an empire off you." In the course of their artistry, Dead Prez addresses such issues as public schools, police brutality, the prison-industrial complex, the preferred way to begin a romance, healthful diets, guerilla warfare, Cointelpro, political prisoners, the situation of activists like Mumia Abu Jamal and Assata Shakur, as well as crass materialism in hip-hop, most vividly on "Radio Freq" (2004). In the liner notes to *Revolutionary but Gangsta* (2004), they promulgate the five-point, RBG Code, which involves the principle of no snitching; the protection of self, family, and community; a commitment to positive education; the initiative to build organizations; and the drive to be productive overall. So all is not bleak. The duo even reflects upon moments of happiness amid the storm; the tune "Happiness" (2000) samples Mayfield's "Be Happy."

While Dead Prez veers to the left, though not so far as not to be able to land on TV, the left edge of rap undoubtedly is set by underground artist Immortal Technique. He covers much of the same thematic territory as Dead Prez, featuring guest spots by Mumia and samples from Malcolm X in the process, but his political vision is described more succinctly and explicitly. On "The Poverty of Philosophy" (2001), he espouses sentiment that could have come from West, as he expresses regret that theorizing about socialist democracy and mobilizing accordingly usually fall beyond the concern of urban Latinos and African Americans struggling to obtain food, clothing, and shelter. Immortal Technique proceeds to hold forth on issues of plutocracies, class exploitation, colonization, economic imperialism, genocide, puppet democracies, fake liberal politicians, conspicuous consumption, social lethargy, house Negroes, and revolution. On "The Prophecy" (2001)—what could be more prophetic?—he rhetorically casts his lot with the proletariat and vows to "trample and dismantle your capitalist philosophy." "The Fourth Branch" (2003) is as close as we get in hip-hop to a Gramscian analysis of corporate media. Gramsci considered the media to be a component of civil society as distinct from state society. In other words, the media were not officially a part of the government apparatus and enjoyed a certain autonomy in their own mission to create a hegemonic bloc. However, Gramsci knew that the cleavage between the two sectors was never total, and that state society would exert direct control over civil society when it deemed such action warranted. In the conception of Immortal Technique, the Gramscian nightmare has been realized because corporate media have become the fourth branch of government, as much a part of the state apparatus as legislative, executive, and judicial operations.

Naturally, a prophetic demonstration of hip-hop by the likes of Dead Prez and Immortal Technique, and to some extent Talib Kweli, is not without its defects. The penchant for mad-aggressive battle verses is still apparent, some, in the case of Immortal Technique, even misogynist and homophobic. To cultivate and maintain audiences, they cannot totally break genre. Yet, the non-sell-out truths that they do spit should be listened to seriously.

So should the music of Jean Grae, the featherweight rapper with the sometimes heavyweight message. One of the most skilled rappers in the game, Grae is a recent addition to the line of female rappers, extending back to MC Lyte, who have tried to thrive in a male-dominated discursive arena and have become somewhat gendered as male in the process.[6] In hip-hop, women in their full dimensions—and full voicings—have been mostly absent. As Toni Blackman writes in "The Feminine Voice in Hip Hop":

they know
i am here

because
i was there

i embraced
the music
as he
did

i rocked
the mic
as he
did

i bore
hip hop
as he
did

we/nurtured
it

(*101*)

Yet, a complex female corporeal presence has been displaced, "made invisible" in Blackman's terms (102). Nonetheless, she vows, "i'll be/ damned/if I/won't/be heard" (102)—thus the challenge for Blackman and artists like Jean Grae. Can they help to stabilize a feminine, even feminist, component in hip-hop?

In the matter of Grae's potential impact, the answer is always maybe. Like prophetic male counterparts Talib Kweli and Immortal Technique (she's recorded with both), she cannot operate totally outside of a genre that demands overblown, self-aggrandizing, boasting lyrics, aggressive battle rhymes, wild party verses, and traces, at the very least, of misogyny and homophobia. So in a sense, one can only pass the Hennessey and listen to her deploy some of her "googleplex of verbal text" to those ends. On the other hand, Jean Grae is a perceptive social critic (wouldn't properly represent her X-men moniker and underground status if she weren't) who critiques corporate hip-hop and the objectification of women. Moreover, her brilliance reaches lyrical and soulful peaks on tracks like the hauntingly poignant "Love Song" (2002), which signifies on "Stop, Look, and Listen," the 1970s hit by the Stylistics, and "Supa Love" (2004). Moreover, on "Block Party" (2002), Grae speaks directly back to Gaye. Regarding the soul singer's classic inquiry, she describes a scenario of black political and moral impotence, a state of affairs that can only be transcended by proper education. In other words, Jean Grae speaks to what Yvonne Bynoe, author of *Stand and Deliver*, calls the "inner work" that remains to be done in the black community (191). The rapper sounds quite Cosbyesque at points, but we should always keep a conversation about black social failings wedded to structural analyses. As Bynoe notes, concerning inner work, "A large portion of this work involves more clearly delineating which negative aspects of our collective existences result from systematic racial discrimination and which factors are caused by our own group inertia, lack of leadership, and the misguided decisions of individuals" (191–92). Jean Grae already recognizes, however, that certain assertions of agency need not and must not be deferred until the resolution of systemic inequalities.

Kanye West, given his unique combination of megasales, ability to command strong production values, high media profile, linguistic creativity, inclination and sometimes willingness to speak forthrightly, and musical ability to find a party beat that can shoulder a message, is the one rapper best positioned at the moment to carry hip-hop's prophetic banner before a mass audience. It's a tall order to retain artistic integrity (assuming you start with some) in the corporate world. As Immortal Technique warns on "The Poverty of Philosophy," "It's not you who will change the system, but the system that will change you." And at points, Kanye does reflect ambivalence about including super-ficial—money, ho's, rims—strokes, or "ice raps," on his rather large artistic canvas. But his critical and prophetic side, as well as spiritual-blues impulse and soul stirrings, loom large on cuts from *The College Dropout* (2004), such as, "All Falls Down," "Spaceship," "Jesus Walks," "Slow Jamz," and "Family Business," and on tracks from *Late Registration* (2005) like "Heard 'Em Say," and "Touch the Sky," on which the lyrics ride atop Mayfield's music from "Move On Up." The one definite about Kanye (folks already whisperin 'bout they wanna hear some *graduation*) is that his fifteen minutes, too, shall pass—which returns us to the question of hip-hop's soul and long-term future.[7]

Essentially, when a critic like Watkins worries about the future of what he calls the hip-hop movement, the trepidation is both admirable and slightly flawed conceptually. Hip-hop is not a movement; it is a racial, ethnic, class, gender, age, and ideological constellation. This kaleidoscopic set of demographics precludes a political formation tied strictly to cultural taste that could be called anything as focused as a movement. Logically, political movements are more defined by objectives and outcomes. Although R&B proved important to the Civil Rights Movement, the political formation, defined by the pursuit of specific legal rights, was indeed called the Civil Rights Movement and was one that involved various cultural constituencies of which R&B aficionados were only one. The political formation was not called the R&B Movement.[8] The thing to angle for, as Cornel West understands, as does Watkins ultimately, in our "necessary engagement with youth culture," is to widen the influence of hip-hop's prophetic faction.[9]

Bigger Than Hip-Hop

The prophetic side of hip-hop is what Geneva Smitherman primarily celebrates in *Word from the Mother: Language and African Americans*. Although she voices support for West's engagement with the hip-hop generation, she resists a conceptual divide that he would make between Constantinian and prophetic, or as expressed in some of its more popular analogs: gangsta versus conscious and booty/bubblegum versus political. She thinks such distinctions are an "illusory dichotomy, emanating from old-line bourgeois thinking" (97). Rejecting an instrumentality versus pure-art debate that recalls those of earlier periods of black cultural politics, she argues, "Hip Hop, like other Black cultural productions, such as literature, is first and foremost art. It has to be assessed not by whether it is 'Gangsta' or 'Conscious,' 'Booty,' 'Bubblegum,' or 'Political,' but by the aesthetic accomplishment (or lack of such) of the Hip Hop artist" (98). I hate to adjudicate this one—no colleague has meant more to me over the course of my career than Smitherman, and I understand that her argument involves a defense of rap artists in touch with the blues impulse against self-righteous or hypocritical attacks from members of an older generation, many of whom have consumed their share of profane, very bawdily blue art. Smitherman herself wonders, "Can Hip Hop resolve its contradictions? Is it not possible for artists to dispense social critique and still pay the rent?" (89). But a satisfactory discussion of contemporary rap music cannot be pursued if one dismisses all criticisms of gangsta as generational and bourgeois. Although it may be true that hip-hop is first and foremost art, it is also true that art itself is first and foremost discourse and circulates as such. The specific manner in which any rap song circulates, which is related to its embracing or eschewing of bubblegumism or the political, is certainly a fair topic for progressive-minded people of any generation. Furthermore, *assessment* as such was not the focal point of the cultural debates to which Smitherman alludes. The controversy centered on *production*, on what African American artists should be doing. People spent less time talking about existing art than arguing about what type of art should come into existence. And on this point, I do agree with her wholeheartedly: debates like those be overly prescriptive and tiresome. Nonetheless, to try to turn the critical clock back to the zenith of New Criticism, straight aesthetics no chaser (which is really some old-school stuff), only serves to undermine a vibrant and variegated dialogue that needs to ensue continually concerning rap music and its reception.

Fortunately, these ruminations by Smitherman are but a miniscule fraction of a nonpareil body of work on African American Language (AAL), including such additional titles as *Talkin That Talk* and the classic *Talkin and Testifyin*. In a subsequent conversation with me about the line of argument put forth in *Word from the Mother*, she further clarified her remarks.[10] She stressed that fundamental to her thinking about the status of hip-hop artists is a sense that certain conceptions of commercial success need to be redefined, that platinum status should not be the only goal or benchmark. She maintained that progressive content can be marketed independently at a level whereby artists can sustain themselves financially—if artists can accept a moderate, and by no means impoverished, definition of "sustain." In short, in answer to her question, she feels that social critics can indeed pay the rent. Trade-offs beyond the level of paying rent are more about greed than material survival.

In any event, Smitherman is the doyenne among scholars who have legitimated the study of AAL, and by extension hip-hop, in academe. In recent years, she has devoted, as a professor, significant classroom time to the study of rap lyrics, discerning not only their strictly linguistic value but also their superior merits as a discursive tool for shaping exploration, knowledge, and critique relative to modern life. She has been joined in this effort by language scholars like Marcyliena Morgan, *Language, Discourse, and Power in African*

American Culture; Gwendolyn Pough, *Check It While I Wreck It*; H. Samy Alim, *Roc the Mic Right* and *You Know My Steez*; and Elaine Richardson, *Hiphop Literacies*.

In the final analysis, for compositionists, the question is how do we—and our students—think about a soundtrack for social progress amid rap music's prevalence? What Socratic pose do we strike toward rap even as we celebrate it? How do we respond to raw descriptions and pronouncements or the assertion, often attributed to Chuck D, that "rap music is black folks' CNN?"[11] Perhaps an initial step is to consider how CNN actually operates. Far from being neutral reporters of all available news, it makes calculated decisions about the news that it makes available and how it will make it available. So if rap music is really to operate like CNN, instead of like CEO, then it ought to make calculated decisions that would do well to emulate the moral framing that Mayfield employed on *Superfly*. Provide the raw stuff; we always need to hear it. But also include formulations that connect that rawness to systems of oppression. All sorts of things go on in the 'hood that don't make it onto rap records but should if the goal truly is to keep it real. What if for every song we get about moving weight, we got one about composition practices? That may sound like a funny question, but think of all the students from the 'hood and the waves of suburban consumers of hip-hop who are subjected to them in composition classrooms. Imagine nuanced, complex, more-than-expressivist, politically sophisticated, worthy, twenty-first-century versions of Langston Hughes's "Theme for English B." Surely we have CNN-style student reporters astute enough to produce them. Imagine employing a sophisticated hermeneutic in studying the choices that writers make, an Aretha Franklin or a Talib Kweli, relative to language use, social prescription, and moral imperative? What issues of artistic integrity or compromise arise? How is a lyricist's attempt to negotiate various discourses instructive for student writers today? How might one further comparative study of Mayfield and contemporary artists and writers? Such inquiries are certainly relevant to critical literacy, and they certainly represent investigation that all the latter-day winners we know can undertake. And imagine, keeping in mind that the era of rap music is almost four times longer than the high-water period of soul music, that some student and/or artist can be inspired by the spirituals and figure out a double-voiced way to get consistently past the guardians of corporate rap.

6
Landing Song

WHEN I sat in a graduate seminar at Columbia University more than thirty years ago, our guest Toni Morrison told us that we should all become better poets than Homer because we get to read Homer while he doesn't get a chance to read us. My ambition never ran that high. Working in the Odyssey Program was probably the closest I will ever get to Homer. If I can just surpass earlier versions of Keith Gilyard, I'll be satisfied. Nevertheless, I think I grasped Morrison's point: read it all, or at least as much as possible; consider all the models to the extent that you can; experiment diligently; practice with discipline; and you never know what potential for craft or for living you may discover inside yourself or generate. The spin I put on it now is that Morrison was speaking about the value of a liberal education and the development of citizens, some of whom will be citizen-poets, in whose hands will be considerable power and influence relative to the fate of American society. Liberal education, it follows, with composing at the heart of it, remains central to the public good and should, therefore, be central to the work of the university. It is in this sense that composition studies, or rhetorical education more broadly, extends beyond the issue of how argument is constituted and constitutes an argument for a more perfect, deeper democracy.

That is the ideal. Of course, how well liberal education thrives is directly related to how far we have traveled down the path of the academic-industrial complex. As investigative reporter Jennifer Washburn describes in *University, Inc.*, market forces have increasingly dictated campus activities over the past quarter century. In a world in which students are often referred to as consumers or clients, and educational efforts are considered "products" and "deliveries," much time and energy have been consumed with franchise deals, licensing agreements, patent negotiations, start-up investments, and market-driven research initiatives. In Washburn's estimation, the problem is not market reality in and of itself. After all, many of our students aspire to a place in the market and pursue education with that goal in mind. To Washburn, the difficulty lies in the "elimination of any clear boundary lines separating academia from commerce" (x). This means that market values seize more control of campuses, the wealth-potential fields of science and technology are overly valorized, and the commercially unprofitable social sciences and humanities tend to be downsized. However, Washburn contends that although the university is used in many ways toward external and extrinsic ends, we should not lose sight that "the source of its greatest strength lies not in its ability to generate commercial products, but in its capacity to appreciate the intrinsic value of intellectual discovery, human creativity, knowledge, and ideas." (240). Ironically, her closing argument suggests the value to business of market-free intellectual inquiry. She points out that the painstaking work of Stanford University's Paul Berg, the Nobel Prize–winning biologist, which made possible the billion-dollar biotech revolution, was not—and would not have been—sponsored primarily by industry because an immediate pay-off was not apparent to venture capitalists. This leads Washburn to question whether future scientists working in academe will enjoy the freedom, unfettered by commercialism, necessary to pursue developments like Berg. Her answer: "Only, it seems, if universities cling to their traditional ideals and maintain their independence from the marketplace. Only, that is, if higher education is appreciated not only for its potential use value but for its intrinsic worth" (241).

Composition instructors, though obviously not simply for business purposes, must remain prominent among those arguing the case. Most of those referenced in this monograph already are, having embraced, in the manner of Cornel West, the intrinsic value of Socratic commitment as ethical educational practice, prophetic witness as motivation for transformative educational and political practice, and tragicomic hope as a reminder of the pedagogical and political resources residual in popular culture. Their work is reflective of psychologist William C. Perry Jr.'s influential discussion of liberal education in *Forms of Intellectual and Ethical Development in the College Years: A Scheme*, particularly as that discussion is interpreted for composition by Patricia Bizzell in "William Perry and Liberal Education." Perry describes movement from student-as-dualist, one attracted to absolutes, authority, and quantification, to student-as-relativist, one unshackled from absolutism but stressing individualism and ahistoricism, to student-as-committed-relativist, one steeped in a self-reflective habit of mind that involves a measured assessment of values in broad historical and communal contexts as both part of and prelude to social decision making. Bizzell, while eschewing, as she should, the strict, Piaget-style, "stage aspects" of Perry's taxonomy and resisting any easy attempt to apply his psychological schema directly to writing curriculums, nonetheless appreciates that Perry has provided a "sort of philosophical map of the sort of changes that liberal education seeks to induce in our students" (453).

At a time when the quality of public discourse has sunk dangerously low, when public leadership is often anti-intellectual and media punditry is mostly pejorative, the need for a liberally educated, critically literate populace has never been greater. Rhetorical education, as I have tried to demonstrate, has a major role to play in fostering the measure of critical literacy that we require. It has a major role to play in elevating the conversations that permeate higher education today and connecting those discussions to the public interest, not only to the unavoidable demands of corporations. Trying to foster critical language awareness in students, with all the examination of discourse, production of text, and preparation for enlightened citizenship implied, is mostly what I mean when I pronounce, "I do composition." And so we return.

> KEITH GILYARD: Cornel, after inviting you formally into composition studies, I want to go back, for framing, to an old question relative to philosophy, rhetoric, and literacy. I'm thinking of Plato's criticism of rhetoric and literacy, that is, the view that those tools were inadequate vis-à-vis a dialectical quest for Truth. I don't want to linger on that argument; the scale of the modern world, among other factors, complicates it. But because philosophical speculation, dialogue, rhetorical performance—somewhat

poetic at that—and writing are all major activities for you as a highly visible scholar, speaker, and teacher, I wonder how you conceptualize the relationships among your writing and publishing, your public appearances, and your formal teaching. Is there, for example, a current philosophy-rhetoric or philosophy-poetry split with which you wrestle?

CORNEL WEST: You got a whole lot in that query. Let me begin by this, though. As you know, my own perspective is that I am aspiring to be a bluesman in the world of ideas, a jazzman in the life of the mind. Therefore, from the very beginning, I have a very distinctive view of that line, 607b in book 10 of Plato's *Republic*, the traditional quarrel between philosophy and poetry. As you know, Plato was trying to displace Homer and the Homeric conception of paideia, that deep education, that formation of attention from the frivolous to the serious, from the trivial to the substantial, that cultivation of a self that has to come to terms with history and memory and mortality and that maturation of a soul. Homer falls short. Plato's philosophical project—dialectic over rhetoric, argument over deployment of tropes, and so on—is the best way to go, especially for sustaining a polis. Now, because I begin as bluesman, it means, then, for me, that the philosophical is certainly going to be one element within the overarching weaponry. The poetic is going to be a crucial element in the overarching weaponry. But, see, music in some ways transcends that. You know, it reminds me in some ways of Richard Strauss's last opera, *Capriccio*. The whole opera is about which is greatest, instrumental music, music with words, or poetry. And at the very end, the voice, European woman's voice, is deeper than all of that. And this is at the very end of the European tradition of opera from Monteverdi to Strauss. Well, black folk begin there. We begin with the human voice and our bodies. That's the only thing we had control over. We had no political power, no economic power for the most part, very little social power even to sustain our families and take care of our kids under the American social death of slavery. So the only thing we had control over was the voice and our bodies in time and space—how we walked, how we talked, how our bodies related. And therefore the human voice took on this unbelievable weight and gravitas for sustaining our sanity and dignity and humanity. And that's the tradition that I come out of, you see? The human voice is at the center.

GILYARD: I understand, a sort of existential declaration, your blue notes as truth rather than simply being a way to mediate truth. But that doesn't get you out of *rhetoric* as many of us employ the term today, that is, in the sense of purposeful symbolic activity operating, as you say, in time and space. You are speaking, actually, of rhetorical moves people make with music. But I do get your vocabulary.

WEST: When we get European instruments, we're going to vocalize them, and we're going to percussionize them. We have Art Tatum on piano or John Coltrane using all those saxophones, which are instruments from Belgium. So this is a profound tradition that is in interaction with, conversant with, Plato's grand dichotomies and dualisms. But as part of a modern people created beneath modernity, but defining the best of modernity, namely black folk in America, I have a deep suspicion of the philosophy on the one side and the usual conception of rhetoric on the other, and so on. You know Nietzsche talks about a danceable education. Give me a Socrates who dances. A God who dances. A gay Socrates. And you say, "Well, Nietzsche, the enslaved Africans, those Africans who were wrestling with bondage had to create a danceable education. A danceable paideia. A singable paideia. A vocalizable paideia." Well, see, that's me. That's me right there.

GILYARD: Ironically, in talking about danceable and vocalizable, you went to the section in *Zarathustra* about reading and writing.[1] But that's partly the point. You're not really grappling intensely with dichotomies but incorporating rather easily your verbal activities within a synthesizing vision, thus your blues and jazz metaphors.

WEST: But the problem is that to conceptualize it within the dominant Western forms means "He must be just a preacher. He must be just a performer. He must be just an entertainer." Well, it depends on what you *mean* by entertainer. Horace said what? "There's delight and instruction."[2] You see? So it's not just stimulating at a superficial level. Right? It depends on what you mean by preacher. Preachers are not just some prerational beings who merely emote. These are some highly sophisticated and intelligent folk musically expressing themselves with intellectual content, with performance, to do what? To make sure these people don't kill themselves and hate themselves and give up on themselves and don't love their children and so forth. So you have to be able to speak at that deepest level, coming out of the African traditions that end up being transformed and transforming in the modern world.

GILYARD: So your public appearances, your public teaching as preaching, or vice versa, this is often the effect for which you are striving, working out of African and African American traditions.

WEST: That's true. Absolutely. And part of it is just being true to yourself. And when I say that Sarah Vaughn and John Coltrane are artistic geniuses, this is not some compliment that has tribalistic overtones. We're talking about human beings who, at the deepest level of their spirit and soul and bodies, were rooted in these traditions of unbelievably refined craft and mastered that craft to impose a structure of feeling and meaning on the world in the whirlwind of white supremacy in which they found themselves. Beethoven is a lot like that. In *Listening to Reason*, Michael Steinberg tells the whole story of German subjectivity from *The Magic Flute* of Mozart to Mahler's symphonies. But Beethoven is at the center. So instead of Kant, Hegel, and Nietzsche, you got Mozart, Beethoven, Brahms, and Mahler. Well, we need to do more of that in the Western world. Because I think Beethoven is much deeper than Hegel. But philosophers will think, "Well, what do you mean, what do you mean?" But I say this because music has been marginalized. Well, what happens when you end up with a people for whom music becomes a privileged site for their definition of who they are in their world because it's against the law for them to read and write? And when they do steal away and learn how to read and write, they still have to relate musically to the folk in order to inspire them, in order to empower, enable, and ennoble them.

GILYARD: As I have been suggesting, there's a decidedly rhetorical function of music at work here. And there's a musicality of rhetoric that those black rhetors had to master. They just had to—

WEST: Exactly—

GILYARD: Or they would have had no audience.

WEST: Especially if they were concerned about those folk. They could go off and be some isolated Negro, convincing white folk that black people had the capacity to think and all that kind of mess, you see? But that's never been part of my tradition—as a choice for me.

GILYARD: Right.

WEST: So that's a long way of saying that when you say a bluesman in the world of ideas and jazzman in the life of the mind, you are relating to Platonic splits between philosophy and rhetoric and so forth. And you understand the poetic in terms of that which intelligently recognizes the limits of critical intelligence. So you're not trashing intelligence; you just know it has limits, and you're willing to acknowledge that. You see? And then when you bring the music in, it's not just the limits of intelligence that is at issue; it's the limits of words. I mean, Victor Hugo defines music, you remember, as "when words fail, but you can't remain silent." So what are you going to do? Well, you fill it with music. And usually, and this is where Vico comes in, very important in this regard, even though the early Rousseau makes the same point, the first utterances of human beings tend to be wrestling with forms of death. So it's lamentation. They're guttural. They're visceral. You see? Why? Because at these funerals, at the death of your loved one, words fail. And yet, you can't just stand there and be silent completely. So you gotta let something out. What do you let out? It's just a guttural cry. And you can transfigure it. So you give it a form. You give it a ritual. So there's somebody singing, but you are singing from your soul. We don't want no cerebral song! This is Momma in that grave! You know what I mean? We want something concrete, substantive. We want something real. You can be out of tune if you want to, but it had better have some depth to it. We don't want perfect pitch and no soul! Everybody loved Momma! You know what I mean? Come on, now!

GILYARD: No doubt. Pathos had better be on display when Momma goes. Logic and character all are bound up with it.

WEST: Well, see, for black folk, you know, we have been on intimate terms with death: social death of American slavery; civic death of Jim Crow, Jane Crow; the psychic death of self-hatred, self-violation; spiritual death of wrestling with hopelessness, meaninglessness, lovelessness. How are people so close to all these forms of death wrestling everyday? It's no accident that the music at this deepest level not just speaks to but helps sustain and has intellectual content; it has a passionate content. You are part of the same tradition in terms of your own work, you know. It's a grand tradition, man. But I'm sorry to go so long on that one question.

GILYARD: It's all right. I wanted to get all of that in place. I'm still trying to develop my sense of how your conceptions of language play out from day to day and how they become translatable into statements about composition pedagogy.

WEST: Your notion of rhetorical education, I think, is probably the best that composition studies can do to capture the complexity of bluesmen and blueswomen in the life of the mind. And I say that in all appreciativeness because all of us are in disciplines that have conceptual limitations. We are trying to generate these paradigms or conceptual schemes that catch fish that continually jump out of those nets. You see? It's hard to find enough sophisticated frameworks to do justice to the doings and sufferings of, say, black people. So theorizing about rhetorical education is the best way, I think, of getting at what's going on, that is, given a view from inside the sophisticated discipline of composition. You know what I mean? It's like the way I come out of pragmatism. I mean, Dewey and these folk hadn't thought about the doings and sufferings of black people at all. They're very useful. They're very important. They'll take you down the road some. Marxism is the same way.

GILYARD: Yeah, well, this is one thing I want to ask you, given what you now know about composition studies—

WEST: Which is still very little. I know your work and a few others. I'm relatively ignorant still—

GILYARD: Composition includes attempts to make pragmatism relevant to pedagogy. Roskelly and Ronald's *Reason to Believe* is the best example I can think of at the moment. They refer to you quite a lot there. Here, as a matter of fact, I have the book right here. My copy is marked up, but I'll send you a clean one. They refer to you quite a bit. So this book is sort of the best example to date, though I don't want to forget about Gilles and Royer or Flower, other people trying explicitly to connect pragmatism to composition practices.[3] So, I would just ask, thinking about composition a little bit, using pragmatism as a starting point, could you extend, in as direct a way as you can manage, the discussion between yourself and compositionists? I'd argue that it's been going on all the time anyway, though not really as a dialogue.

WEST: It's a beautiful thing to know. You educated me in so many different ways on different levels. But I'm astonished at the degree to which they find use. I'm glad they do. Well, I think that pragmatism is always useful within the Western philosophical tradition because it is so subversive of precisely the kind of dualisms and dichotomies that we began with, with Plato, and we see similar kinds of moves in Aristotle. And Christian theology often imitates and emulates the Greeks in this regard. With pragmatism, you really get the stress on social practices and a stress on fallibilism and contextualism. You get the centrality of agency—always under structural constraints—but agency nonetheless: the doing, the thinking as a form of doing, a stress on consequences and effects as opposed to origins and beginnings. So history becomes crucial. And the future—almost a metaphysical status ascribed to futurity—the future can be different. Human beings can make the present different in such a way that a new future can come into being. That, to me, is very useful.

GILYARD: And useful to composition instructors as well. I think more and more of them, at least I hope so, are deriving their instructional goals from such a sense of agency and possibility—though there can be an agency of avoidance.

WEST: The problem of pragmatism, for me, has always been that it emerges within a European secular context in which a sensitivity to issues of what Du Bois would call spiritual striving at the deep level are alluded to, referred to but not lingered on for long. So the issues of death, dread, disappointment, disenchantment, disillusionment, and nihilism are not emphasized. Dewey is the greatest example. But this brother right here (*pointing to bookshelf*), Giacomo Leopardi, is one of my soul mates, the greatest lyrical poet of early-nineteenth-century Europe. He's from Italy, so he doesn't get a lot of play. There's Dante, Petrarch. Leopardi dies at thirty-eight years old. Catch the blues, man! Oh, he's powerful! Remember in the *Cornel West Reader* I used his poetry as juxtaposition with spirituals?

GILYARD: I remember that. Actually, I saw the comparison when it appeared in the original piece, which you did as a foreword for Richard Newman's collection of spirituals.[4]

WEST: That brother Leopardi is so deep. But he begins with "the mind's sweet shipwreck."[5] That's how he starts. You see? But Dewey never gets there. Critical intelligence for Dewey is always so productive. And I argue with my dear brother Eddie Glaude on this because he's a kind of blues-inflicted Deweyan.[6] He's got creative tensions, you know. I tell him, "Well, no. Dewey did not get there." Not to "the mind's sweet shipwreck," you see? Leopardi begins with critical intelligence in shipwreck, whereas for Dewey, even if that's a moment, he's not going to stay too long.

GILYARD: So let me get this straight. It's not just the restrained politics in Dewey, which you have written about, that you find too narrow. It's his idea of critical intelligence itself.

WEST: Well, you see, for black folk, we begin in shipwreck, literally on the ship and, symbolically, dealing with white supremacy, looking at the abyss. So we have the issue of spiritual striving. And this is why Du Bois begins *The Souls of Black Folk* with "The Crying of Water." You remember? And then "Nobody Knows the Trouble I've Seen." That's how he starts the whole text. "The Crying of Water," from Arthur Symons, European poet, and then "Nobody Knows." So you begin, then, in the limited situation, right on the edge of the abyss.

GILYARD: So how do you square that? Because you always have maintained that Du Bois lacked a sense of the tragic. Or maybe you said that he lacked a sense of the absurd. But I think the import is the same either way. And, knowing all that Du Bois had to deal with, I've always been a little puzzled by your contention. I couldn't quite tease that out.

WEST: It's a tough thing. I think that Du Bois is just so rich, so deep, so profound. But I think of the chapter on the death of his son.

GILYARD: "On the Passing of the First-Born."

WEST: Exactly. He comes close. But even there he doesn't want to linger.

GILYARD: It's the shortest essay in the book.

WEST: He doesn't want to just acknowledge the concrete body in the coffin. His dead son becomes a moment for greater freedom. He becomes the instance . . . nah, this ain't no "instance or moment." He in the coffin, man! Look! Look! Look! Stay with it, man! Last year he was breathing, laughing. He dead now! See what I mean? This ain't no scheme for the end or the aim. See what I mean? There's got to be a moment of candid confrontation with the corpse. Because death ain't no concept. It's not an abstract thing. Now, what do you do with the direct concrete thing? That's where spirituality comes in, the song, the holding hands of the loved one, and the acknowledgment of shipwreck. Ain't no explanation. It's an absurd in the universe—a black hole in our world of meaning. It's absurd on a certain level. So even the Christians come along, "Well, it's just God who got a overarching"—No! Kiss my black behind! No! If that's the kind of God we dealing with, you see, then all these Africans need to die in order for God to get the project in place? Nope. That ain't the kind of God we talking about. We have to understand that this is a mystery. This is absurd in the universe. It's a hole in the universe. And it's absurd when you try to couch it in terms of critical intelligence. And of course, when Dewey's baby died, he went silent, man. Now, I would say to Dewey—and I love John Dewey—"You know, let's start your project with the death of your child." In fact, in some ways, a major part of my critique of the academy is that it so manicures and deodorizes and sanitizes the catastrophic and traumatic. The academy tries to flatten all of that out so it could be skated over as students come in. Of course, the irony is the students come in damaged souls, wounds, bruises, scars, and they think education is about escaping all of that.

GILYARD: Well, we get a lot of that perspective. Those are our composition classrooms. We get almost all of the students.

WEST: That's right, because of the required courses.

GILYARD: We have near-universal status that way.

WEST: Absolutely. So they, early on, have to be taught how they'll be socialized into this subculture of the college and university. And thank God they got professors like yourself and a few others out there who are saying, "You know what? This is not an escape from life. This is an engagement with life. So you think you're getting away from the traumatic by going to school because a school is this manicured, deodorized place. No. You are getting weaponry. Socratic weaponry. Prophetic weaponry—

GILYARD: Right. There you go. Prophetic pragmatism coming out as pedagogy—

WEST: —to engage the world and try to make it a little better before you die. Because you gonna die. You can stay in school all you want; you still gon die. Your momma gon drop dead; your girlfriend gon betray you, maybe. All those things everybody gotta go through." You see? And it's a beautiful thing to see the critical theorists and the radical pragmatists and those followers of Paulo Freire and bell hooks and others in composition because in some ways you all are on the front line when it comes to the socialization of the students into the subculture of academic, critical discourse.

GILYARD: Oh yeah, we collectively are keepers at a major gate, one way or another, no question. But the people on watch vary continually, so you don't know if the critical will always be privileged.

WEST: Well, you see, that's one of the reasons I teach a freshman seminar every year.

GILYARD: Okay. I want to get back to your teaching a little later, but I want to ask you about faith matters now while the topic is on my mind given some of what you have said about souls. In rhetorical education—well, I mention it in the text, right?—religion is an increasingly important topic in classrooms. Based on your experiences, how would you advise teachers about how to deal with students concerning rhetoric and religion or even the rhetoric of religion?

WEST: I think that it has to be confronted and engaged, critically examined. I think the last thing you want to do is not allow the students to bring in their own theological baggage, their own religious assumptions and presuppositions. It's just that—and you say this with great insight and eloquence in the text—that when you bring it into the public conversation, it has to be Socratic all the way down. You have to have a critical examination of the Christian, the Islamic, the Judaic, the secular, the agnostic, the atheistic, across the board. But it has to be done in such a way that people feel as if they are embodied persons who are being challenged, so that the arguments are not viewed as just disembodied abstractions that don't affect how they live. Anytime people are talking about religion, if they're believers, these are the most precious, delicate issues of life and death, and joy and sorrow, and pain and grief and pleasure. That's part of the conscientization that brother Paulo Freire talked about. The same is true in regard to the political dimension. It has to do with folks just having been told lies. White supremacy is a lie. And yet racism is so pervasive. So it's going to be painful to acknowledge that your pastor lied to you. Your momma and daddy have been lying to you. But that doesn't mean you don't love them anymore. They are part of a whole larger system, too. But that's going to be painful. And the only way that pain is real is when people feel as if those claims are tied to them. If we are distant from it, if it's just disembodied, then we could just act as if it doesn't affect us at all. And the end and aim, really, are maturation, cultivation, and deep education, which have everything to do with awakening.

GILYARD: Right. You mention Paulo Freire, and I'm reminded of the dialogue that he had with Myles Horton.

WEST: Oh yes.

GILYARD: *We Make the Road by Walking.* Horton recalled a tour he was on with Saul Alinsky and how they had a little disagreement because Alinsky was saying that organizing sort of preceded education, that organizing educates. And Horton's position was that you had to educate to organize, that education made organizing possible. Alinsky was like, "No, you organize. Education comes out of the organizing." I don't think Myles Horton pushed the distinction that hard, but he kept it as a split in his mind because it helped him to conceptualize what he was doing at Highlander Folk School.[7] But I think in composition we have a lot of people, you know, who buy into this notion of critical pedagogy, a lot of it drawing on Freire and others. And they say, "Well, I do this critical pursuit in class, and this makes a difference." As you indicate, it does make a difference because we're on the front lines of dealing with students. But there's a tension because some people say, "Well, I do this in class, at the office, so to speak. That's my radical contribution. I gave at the office." Other people are saying, "Well, there isn't but so much you can do in a classroom because a classroom is still on a campus." In other words, some folks are saying that if you're serious about activism, you have to go beyond the classroom. You have to connect, not so much town and gown, but particular instances of town to gown. You have to connect that up in some way—

WEST: Absolutely—

GILYARD: And I was wondering about your take on that because you're both off-campus and on-campus a lot.

WEST: Well, first in relation to Brother Myles Horton and Brother Saul Alinsky. For me, Myles Horton was one of the great existential democrats of the twentieth century in terms of understanding democracy as a way of life. I don't think Alinsky was a deep existential democrat. I think he was preoccupied with power, with winning, with victories. He had deep compassion for working people, but I don't believe that he had the depth that Myles Horton had when it came to trying to radicalize human beings existentially, politically, economically, personally, socially. Myles knew that sometimes it's better to lose and radicalize human beings than to win the victory and in the process develop people who are only obsessed with winning, so by the time they do win, they're just acting the same way the elites that they opposed acted. This is because they hadn't been conscientized in that deep way. And Myles understood that. I think. Paulo Freire also understood that. Now, Alinsky's tradition is a great tradition, and I should say that IAF [the Industrial Areas Foundation] today, with my dear brother Ernesto Cortés, understands that. But when you look at *Rules for Radicals* and *Reveille for Radicals*, and so forth, you don't get that deeper existential concern that I like in Myles. Now, how does that relate to the second question, which has to do with the difference between the classroom and the street or the church or the community center or trade union hall and so forth? I do think there is a different kind of pedagogy. See, within the classroom, the stress on Socratic paideia is crucial. You're not able to be as explicit and as intense as in the deep-democratic paideia that I would do outside because that can easily become too tendentious or almost indoctrinating within the context of the classroom where you must be open to a variety of perspectives. You got right-wing brothers and sisters, centrists, liberals, so forth and so on. If I speak at the Left Forum, let's say, I can really passionately and critically engage the American empire and lay out policy and lay out what needs to be done and how we ought to go about organizing. But I shouldn't do that in a classroom. That's not the context for that kind of deep-democratic paideia. That's the context for a Socratic paideia. Everybody examines himself or herself. "Let's become more alert, aware. Let's awaken. Let's quit the sleepwalking. Let's muster the courage to think, and let's muster the courage to connect our thinking with empathizing." Now, that's some raw stuff, but that's not the systematic critique of empire that I would lay out with passion as a normative claim. Now, in the Socratic dialogue, I will make known my commitment to the deep-democratic paideia. See? So students say, "Well, we read *Democracy Matters*. This is really going far in terms of your critique, my God!" And I say, "Yeah, and I think I'm right about that, too." That's where my deep-democratic vision takes me, but in classroom conversation, I am involved in a Socratic discussion, though I in no way disavow my connection to the deep-democratic vision.

GILYARD: So the Socratic discussion is only a particular slice or element of your overall strategy.

WEST: But I believe there's a continuum. I don't believe that there's one model or paradigm for this. Some people just don't have a lot of energy. And so if they could just get through the Socratic paideia and make their contributions in terms of unsettling and unnerving students, that's a beautiful thing. I don't believe everybody has to do what I do. I've got a lot of energy. And I like to be in a lot of contexts. And I like to be challenged. But I just have a high metabolism. And I don't believe those of us who have a high metabolism have to say everybody has to do like we do or that it makes us better in that regard. Not at all. All of us have to be true to ourselves. But we do have to recognize what our various strengths are because all of us do have strengths who are involved in this struggle as a whole. Actually, I could learn a lot from people who are masters in the classroom, even though after the classroom is over, they just go on home and take a nap. I can learn a lot from them. They might be able to learn from me, in terms of what I'm doing outside the classroom, in terms of what they could do in the classroom better. Because—

GILYARD: Well, some of them been doing it—

WEST: That's true, from the writings and so forth. So, in that sense, I don't believe in putting down or trashing them or anything like that. I think we all have our own voices, and we just want to be true to our voices. And our callings take different forms, but we're all part of the same larger deep-democratic cause—those who are a part of the critical composition, critical rhetorical tradition that we're talking about.

GILYARD: Well, a lot of what you're hearing in composition classrooms now is this aversion to discussing race. I think out of all your texts, the one that's been most quoted in composition studies has been *Race Matters*. But we're in an era now in which the race-class dynamic is coming up more and more, and students say,

"I've read enough about the black stuff. I'm tired of that. I feel like it's being shoved down my throat. I don't want to hear it."

WEST: Yeah, that's the truth, too, in terms of hearing that complaint. I mean, the thing is that any serious discussion about white supremacy has always acknowledged the role of class and gender and empire. You're not going to have a serious discussion about race unless those elements are in some way acknowledged. But, on the other hand, it's so easy to want to jettison the existential and psychic dimensions of white supremacy, especially because so many white brothers and sisters either are ignorant of them or don't want to wrestle with them. But the labor question and the issue of class and the exploited working-class status of people of color are always already there. And the imperial projects of the capitalist regimes that are exploiting these black and white and red workers are always already there. This is what Du Bois and C. L. R. James and others like Sinclair Drake taught us years ago. I think part of the problem, though, is that it's very difficult for the white mainstream to candidly confront a long history of institutionalized contempt and organized hatred of black people. It's just hard for them to come to terms with that, even our Marxist comrades, some of whom just want to talk about labor exploitation. I say, "Nah, nah, nah, they cut the brother's thing off, man, on a tree." That's not economic exploitation. That's psychosexual dynamics that have to do with a fear of black bodies, that have to do with insecurity regarding black sexuality, especially male, you see. So you have to be true to what is going on. Yes, it's a form of control of labor. No doubt about that. But it's more than that. It's got to be. And if black folk are living it, then you have to be true to our realities. This is not compartmentalized. We are seen as just workers, but they cut Johnson's johnson off. Hey! That's not economic exploitation! They can't come to terms with his sexuality! They fearing something. They insecure. They got anxieties about something. We have to be true to that. And if they doing that on a tree, then they feeling that when the black brother walks on the bus. They feeling that when a black brother walks into the corporate suite. Or when the professor walks into the room. He's a black man. (*Gasps.*) "Oh! Professor Gilyard! Wow! He looks like Luther Vandross's second cousin! I'll be danged!" The image. The body. And then the brilliance comes out. "Wow! He's very articulate." And all that mess comes out. And you say, "Wait a minute, there's something else going on." So we just have to tell our critical-compositional comrades, "Yes, race, class, gender, sexual orientation, and empire are inextricably involved, but they're not identical. Inseparable but not identical. There's a specificity to each one of those, even though they come together in a certain kind of configuration relative to historical moments.

GILYARD: I think I suggested that you should write a book on pedagogy.

WEST: Yeah, you mentioned that.

GILYARD: You should.

WEST: I wouldn't know what to say.

GILYARD: Sure you would.

WEST: I'd tell them to read your book.

GILYARD: No.

WEST: Not just the book on me but your other work also. No, it's true, because you—

GILYARD: No. I'm thinking more and more that you should. I mean, hey, bell hooks did it. She wrote two.

WEST: Oh, bell's powerful, man, you know.

GILYARD: But I think maybe you should at some point. People want to know about liberal arts education these days, especially in a climate where many view education as so privatized, including a lot of the students coming here to Princeton University.

WEST: Absolutely.

GILYARD: And you talk about the democratic paideia, you know, the agora, the notion that education is for the public good. We don't mind some of the career aspirations of students. They got to go get a job, make some money. They want to get paid. But the notion that education is for the public good kind of gets lost in current conversation. So I feel that we have to talk more about liberal education today, sharpen our analyses of its worth and future given the onslaught of market logic on campuses. And then you mentioned that you habitually teach a freshman seminar. So I was wondering about your general musings about liberal education, why you teach what you teach, how your ideas play out in your own classrooms. We already have some sense of that in terms of the Socratic commitment, but how do some of your other ideas about liberal education influence your classroom?

WEST: Part of it is that you don't have a democracy without "we consciousness." See, this invisible-hand conception of democracy, where everybody pursues private goods, and somehow the public interest will be served, is a myth and a lie. I think that you have to have a training ground for citizenship. Citizenship is the moral regeneration and ascent of kinship from tribe and clan. There's a moral ascent to citizen and public interest and public good. And if you don't have citizenship, you are going to end up degenerating into kinship. So you have to have public interest and common good as crucial aspects of your critical reflection. Those concerns are not going to just bubble to the top if everybody's pursuing education for private ends and aims. And yet that's the dominant orientation in our market-driven society. You're absolutely right. Even in the public institutions, you know?

GILYARD: And I would say that public institutions are the main places about which to be concerned.

WEST: But sometimes it's even more difficult—

GILYARD: Yeah—

WEST: Because you're dealing with young populations who are feeling as if they're on the outside and can't wait to get in for the pursuit of those private goods. And more and more of these public institutions are imitating, emulating the private universities as if we have some paradigm of goodness, truth, and beauty, which seems the case because they are successful within the market-driven society as a whole. And this is why I thank God, you know, that as professors, we can still make some crucial choices in terms of what we teach, how we teach, how we go about participating in the training ground for citizenship, the exploration of critical consciousness connected to three dimensions of time. You know, the past, the sense of history; the present, the structural and institutional analyses and existential cultural issues; and the future, the concern about making the future a better place and a radically different place no matter how unpopular the relevant ideas are and no matter how against the grain they are. Which is to say what? Which is to say that, in so many ways, you know especially for somebody like myself, who has been living under death threats for the past fifteen years, the issue of the price to be paid for critical pedagogy is very real. The white-supremacist alliances, especially the organized ones that are explicitly militaristic in their xenophobia, you know, they'll kill you in a minute. They'll shoot you down like a dog. In a second! If their interests are substantively threatened. I don't at the moment threaten their interests in any substantive way. I'm trying to. That's what I'm about. That's my end and aim. You know, if we can get organized by the millions—that's exactly what we are trying to do. They get the point. Ain't no doubt about that. But it means that the issue of courage is important. Courage is the enabling virtue.

GILYARD: Courage and the drive to keep the teaching project critical.

WEST: The way your students say, "Well, Brother West got to come more with it against Foucault." That's a wonderful thing. That's what the challenge is about.

GILYARD: Well, the intellect should rest but not for long. If we are modeling our pedagogy—and we should—we keep seeking challenges.

WEST: You know, I was just with Hugo Chavez because a press in Venezuela is translating *Democracy Matters*.

GILYARD: That's interesting.

WEST: It's part of the literacy program. Yeah, I was down there. And we met for nine hours, man. Dialogue with that brother, man. It was a rich, it was a very rich thing. Because he's fundamentally a Christian like myself. He comes out of liberation theology—

GILYARD: Well, many of the Central American and South American progressives come out of that tradition—

WEST: —connecting the love of Jesus to courage and social justice and to what love looks like in public. So it's this commitment to justice, which is really a part of Hebrew scriptures, too, with Amos and so forth. But it's this attempt to somehow be true to oneself more than anything. And that takes us right back to where we started.

GILYARD: What are you teaching this semester?

WEST: I'm teaching a freshman seminar with Robert George, the conservative brother, the pro-Bush intellectual. I got him reading Du Bois, Gramsci, Marx, and he's got me reading Hayek—of course, I've read Hayek—Leo Strauss, and so forth, the Pope. And it's a wonderful thing. We go back and forth, back and forth. And then I'm teaching a course with Jeff Stout on democracy and religion in America. Of course, we use a lot of King, and, because there's a focus on organizing, we end up reading a lot of

Alinsky. We read Myles Horton; we read Charles Payne, *I Got the Light of Freedom*. We read Ella Baker. Barbara Ransby's book on Ella Baker and the black freedom movement is very important.[8] We read stuff on Stokely. We had read some Emerson, Thoreau, Lincoln, and Douglass as well. And we're going to end up talking about IAF, the Industrial Areas Foundation, with Brother Ernesto Cortés, what they do with the Alinsky stuff because they take it much more into the politics of everyday life regarding religion and culture than Saul did. But it's a wonderful thing. We started with Sheldon Wolin, who was my thesis adviser. I wrote *The Ethical Dimensions of Marxist Thought* under him. Sheldon Wolin, to me, is the greatest theorist of democracy alive. He's about eighty-five years old and a serious, serious radical, towering—

GILYARD: Everybody's towering with you. I think that's your compliment—

WEST: That's my compliment?

GILYARD: That's your adjective.

WEST: My adject—

GILYARD: Towering.

WEST: No, it's true. No, there are a number of them. There are a number. But each one is really towering, though!

GILYARD: Right!

WEST: Oh, Lord! Brother Wolin, *Politics and Vision*, and then the big book on de Tocqueville, *Tocqueville between Two Worlds*. And he wrote that book on the student movement in '64 around Berkeley.

GILYARD: Oh, the Free Speech Movement? I know that book.[9] He was teaching there.

WEST: Absolutely. He has this notion of fugitive democracy where he believes that democracy from below will usually overflow, and then it's repressed and incorporated and absorbed. You have to try it again, and it's repressed and incorporated. You see this flowing back and forth. Wolin's just a magnificent theorist. And he's one of the few Jewish intellectuals who has actually been very honest on the Middle East, telling the truth about the suffering there across borders, across the various ethnic and political lines. But Sheldon Wolin, he's got high status in political theory, but he's not as well known as he ought to be. I mean, I think Wolin is a very important figure for composition studies.

GILYARD: Okay. I'll have to check him out seriously.

WEST: Wolin is very important. He really is. You know, he wrote an essay in 1969 called "Political Theory as Vocation," which is a classic piece that's a critique of the dominant paradigms in political theory and examines how you preserve subversive possibility.

GILYARD: That's where you got one of your titles from, then?

WEST: Oh, the vocation?

GILYARD: Yeah. The piece in your reader that you call "On My Intellectual Vocation." The interview by George Yancy, though I don't know if that is the original title. But the word *vocation* rang the connection in for me as soon as you said it.

WEST: Oh, absolutely. Vocation and invocation! You see? That calling and re-calling. So you can't really have a vocation unless you have the invocation that allows you to re-member and put together what has been dismembered and shattered. And so, your calling is linked to a re-calling, a re-membering, a historical recollection that connects you then to the best of a past.

GILYARD: We can wrap it on that note.

WEST: Are we finished? Look at this piece. It's in a German publication. I gave a lecture a couple months ago in Berlin.

GILYARD: (*reading*) "Von . . . von Cornel West."

WEST: Well, I started off very much with what we were talking about, with the blues, how the blues nation must learn from a blues people or lose our democracy.

Notes, Bibliography, Index

Notes

1. Flight West

1. See, respectively, Lu, "An Essay on the Work of Composition," "Professing Multiculturalism," and "Redefining the Literate Self"; Smitherman, *Word from the Mother*; Kells, *Hector P. Garcia*; Holmes, *Revisiting Racialized Voice*; Fox, *Defending Access* and "Race and Collective Resistance"; Ball and Lardner, *African American Literacies Unleashed*; Okawa, "Removing Masks"; Miller, "The Nervous System"; Crawford, "Building a Theory of Affect in Cultural Studies Composition Pedagogy"; Mutnick, *Writing in an Alien World*; Marback, "From Athens to Detroit," "Corbett's Hand," "Detroit and the Closed Fist," "Ebonics," and "Police Violence and Denials of Race"; Daniell, "Narratives of Literacy"; Destigter, "Good Deeds" and *Reflections of a Teacher Citizen*; Kates, "The Embodied Rhetoric of Hallie Quinn Brown"; Kopelson, "Rhetoric on the Edge of Cunning"; Young, *Minor Re/Visions*; Hesford, *Framing Identities*; Stull, *Amid the Fall, Dreaming of Eden*; Severino, "Two Approaches to 'Cultural Text'"; Soliday, "Translating Self and Difference through Literacy Narratives"; Kynard, "'Trying to Bend the Tree When It Is Already Grown'"; Mailloux, *Reception Histories*; Roskelly and Ronald, *Reason to Believe*; Flower, Long, and Higgins, *Learning to Rival*, and Flower's sections in that book, "An Experimental Way of Knowing" and "The Rival Hypothesis Stance and the Practice of Inquiry," as well as her *CCC* article "Talking Across Difference."

2. At three points in *Democracy Matters*, West refers to parrhesia. The first instance is in reference to Socrates' explanation in Plato's *Apology*: "There, gentleman, you have the true facts, which I present to you without any concealment or suppression, great or small. I am fairly certain that this plain speaking of mine is the cause of my unpopularity, and this really goes to prove that my statements are true, and that I have described correctly

the nature and the grounds of the calumny which has been brought against me" (16, sec. 24a). West's second mention of parrhesia involves his wishes for the media: "There can be no democratic *paideia*—the critical cultivation of an active citizenry—without democratic *parrhesia*—a bold and courageous press willing to speak against the misinformation and mendacities of elites" (39). His third and most extended comment about parrhesia (208–12) suggests how the concept informs political treatises such as Plato's *Republic* and James Madison's *Federalist Papers*. Although several competing conceptions of parrhesia exist, for my purposes the frank questioning of received wisdom remains the heart of the matter. Michel Foucault, in his seminar "Discourse and Truth," which was conducted in 1983 at the University of California at Berkeley, traced the origin of the term in Greek literature to Euripides. Foucault's major objective in this regard was to develop, in his words, "a genealogy of the critical attitude in Western philosophy" as distinct from an "analytics of truth" (*Fearless Speech* [170–71]). Foucault described the function of parrhesia in the ancient Greek world to be opposite that of rhetoric in that the former could entail no deception as could the latter. For a *parrhesiastes*, the subject of the enunciation (the speaking subject), coincided precisely with the subject of *enunciandum*, the belief held. Fundamental to the exercise of parrhesia was courage because it almost always placed the speaker at risk. The frank speech of kings, for example, was not considered an act of parrhesia by Foucault because speaking frankly posed no danger to kings (12–24).

Foucault also recognized a "crisis of the *function* of *parrhesia*" (72), which related to questions of who should be able to use parrhesia, whether frankness alone was the sufficient condition for truth, and how parrhesia should connect, if at all, to mathesis—knowledge and education (72–73). Foucault arrived at his Berkeley comments by way of a long and circuitous process that was reflected in some of his lectures at the College de France in 1982, later published as *The Hermeneutics of the Subject*. First, he drew upon the work Philodemus and explained that for the Epicureans, the frankness of parrhesia was integral to master-disciple or guide-student relationships (137). Later, Foucault noted that if the proper mission of students is to "build up a relationship of sovereignty to themselves, with regard to themselves, typical of the wise and virtuous subject" (385), then their guides, the ones whose practice of parrhesia is fundamental, should deploy parrhesia in a disinterested yet generous manner. In other words, as Foucault expressed it, "Generosity towards the other is at the very heart of the moral obligation of *parrhesia*" (385). Still later, after acknowledging the existence of "a whole range of modalities" relative to parrhesia, he observed that a crucial difference between Greco-Roman and Christian practices of parrhesia was that in the former case, the practice was more akin to pedagogy and depended heavily upon the truth held by the teacher, whereas more important in the latter conception was the truth of another mode, such as scripture, which essentially suppressed quests for personal truth (407–8). I consider Foucault at length here, as well as reflect on the "range of modalities," to make it clear that for my project the mere, no matter how frank, insistence on a particular truth claim is not what I mean by parrhesia. The acknowledgment of power differentials and social injustice, the relationship among parties involved in the discourse (mutual regard as a minimum), and the position of the speaker relative to received wisdom (oppositional or at the very least negotiating) are key elements for me. Moreover, the appeal to a text that is deemed to represent absolute truth, the fundamentalist concept of fearless speech, is not what I regard as parrhesia. In other words, bibliolatry, blind patriotism, or any other dogma, for that matter, are the opposite of parrhesia, particularly in the sense that parrhesia is coupled with Socratic engagement, a connection that is my primary concern here.

2. The Roots of a Deep-Democratic Project

1. In Dewey's essay, see *The Philosophy of John Dewey*, especially 49–51. Dewey added, for example:

> And this change in point of view is almost revolutionary in its consequences. An empiricism which is content with repeating facts already past has no place for possibility and for liberty. It cannot find room for general conceptions or ideas, at least no more than to consider them as summaries or records. But when we take the point of view of pragmatism we see that general ideas have a very different role to play than that of reporting and registering past experiences. They are the bases for organizing future observations and experiences. Whereas, for empiricism, in a world already constructed and determined, reason or general thought has no other meaning than that of summing up particular cases, in a world where the future is not a mere word, where theories, general notions, rational ideas have consequences for action, reason necessarily has a constructive function. Nevertheless the conceptions of reasoning have only a secondary interest in comparison with the reality of facts, since they must be confronted with concrete observations. (50)

2. In his introduction to James's *Pragmatism: A New Name for Some Old Ways of Thinking*, Bryan Vescio refers to the book as the "first self-conscious, thorough, and consistent attempt to explore the implications of pragmatist thinking" (xii). The book contains eight lectures that James delivered at the Lowell Institute in Boston late in 1906, lectures he repeated at Columbia University early in 1907. James, in lecture 2, "What Pragmatism Means," credited Peirce with introducing the term *pragmatism* into philosophy in an 1878 article titled "How to Make Our Ideas Clear." According to James, the formal idea of pragmatism went unnoticed until he reintroduced Peirce's conception in 1898 at Berkeley in a lecture titled "Philosophical Conceptions and Practical Results." James recalls, "Mr. Peirce, after pointing out that our beliefs are really rules for action, said that, to develop a thought's

meaning, we need only determine what conduct it is fitted to produce: that conduct is for us its sole significance. And the tangible fact at the root of all our thought-distinctions, however subtle, is that there is no one of them so fine as to consist in anything but a possible difference of practice. To attain perfect clearness in our thoughts of an object, then, we need only consider what conceivable effects of a practical kind the object may involve—what sensations we are to expect from it, and what reactions we must prepare. Our conception of these effects, whether immediate or remote, is then for us the whole of our conception of the object, so far as that conception has positive significance at all. This is the principle of Peirce, the principle of pragmatism" (20–21).

3. While appreciative of Emerson's achievement, West, in *The American Evasion of Philosophy*, expansively and compellingly critiques Emerson's imperialist sensibility (19–23) and his racism (29–35).

4. West details Hook's shift from Marxist to Cold Warrior (*American Evasion of Philosophy* 114–24), Niebuhr's movement from Christian leftist critic to a similar Cold Warrior posture (*American Evasion of Philosophy* 150–64), and Rorty's narrow political vision that serves, in the end, as an apology for liberal bourgeois capitalism (*American Evasion of Philosophy* 206–07). One could, however, imagine West adopting a softer stance toward Rorty based on a subsequent read of, say, *Achieving Our Country: Leftist Thought in Twentieth-Century America*. In any event, see Christopher J. Voparil, *Richard Rorty: Politics and Vision*, particularly the last two sections, "America as the Greatest Poem" (155–81) and "Rorty and Thesis Eleven" (182–93) for a recent analysis of Rorty's ideas.

5. For original context, see Du Bois, *The Souls of Black Folk*, 5.

6. For expanded comments by Mailloux, see his *Reception Histories*, 40–42, for example: "And true, rhetorical pragmatism claims no necessary, logical connection to any particular political ideology. But still, with its tropes of dialogue and conversation, with its arguments for rhetorical exchange, with its narratives of interpretive debates as the only way to establish truth, sophistic rhetorical pragmatism can promote and be promoted by democratic forms of political organization" (41).

7. In the introduction to the 1995 edition of his book, Ohmann recognizes the problematic nature of his call: "Prescribing socialist revolution as I did raised difficulties of other sorts. The tidy formulation made it sound as if the path toward radical change had been reliably charted already, by theorists or by foreign revolutionaries whose model need only be applied in this society. It left open the questions, what kind of socialism and how might a socialist society make and mobilize knowledge if not through professions like our own. It implied the paralyzing idea that nothing can be changed until everything is changed. It put an intimidating distance between the working lives of the readers I meant to address and the choices I thought they might fruitfully make if they shared my analysis" (xxvi). The later Ohmann says, "There are reforms and reforms; the task is to figure which ones are likely

to be palliative and which ones might open out into broader alliances, more radical change" (xxvi–xxvii).

8. Hobbes does not attribute the continual quest for power only to greed or a desire to rule. On the other hand, he views the impulse to gain more and more power to be sometimes a defensive measure. In other words, if one is not continually gaining power, one might become the victim of someone else's mission to gain power. In either case, the desire for power threatens peace and security and causes fear of oppression, matters obviated by the creation of a commonwealth (160–68), which functions as "that great LEVIATHAN . . . that mortal god to which we owe, under the immortal God, our peace and defence" (223–28).

9. The most concise introduction to Marxist thinking remains *The Communist Manifesto*. The early pages describe the stages of class antagonism and the contradictions that will undo the bourgeoisie (Marx and Engels 34–52). The formation of the revolutionary class, the proletariat, is discussed (46–50). The steps of the predicted revolution are outlined (60–62). For discussion of ideology and consciousness, see *The Communist Manifesto* (58–60), and Marx and Engels, *The German Ideology* (37–72). For more on Marx's materialist conception of history, see *The German Ideology* (48–60); for his ideas about surplus value see parts three, four, and five of *Capital*, and for definitions of key terms, see the reader's guide in *The Portable Karl Marx* (559–73).

10. The basic texts from which West derives his taxonomy are Vladimir Lenin's *What Is to Be Done?* and *One Step Forward, Two Steps Back*; Joseph Stalin's *Foundations of Leninism* and *Concerning Questions of Leninism*; Leon Trotsky's *New Course*; Gramsci's "Workers' Democracy" and "The Modern Prince"; Eduard Bernstein's *Evolutionary Socialism*; Rosa Luxemburg's *Social Reform or Revolution* and "Organizational Questions of Russian Social Democracy"; Anton Pannekoek's "Marxist Theory and Revolutionary Tactics"; and Korsch's "Fundamentals of Socialization."

11. The similar passage in *The German Ideology* reads, "The ideas of the ruling class are in every epoch the ruling ideas, i.e., the class which is the ruling *material* force of society, is at the same time its ruling *intellectual* force. The class which has the means of material production at its disposal, has control at the same time over the means of mental production, so that thereby, generally speaking, the ideas of those who lack the means of mental production are subject to it" (64).

12. Gramsci theorized that there are two levels of superstructure, one he termed "civil society," organizations and institutions that are private for the most part, and the other he called "political society," or the state. Civil society reflects hegemony, whereas political society represents direct domination or command. Officials of the dominant group are "deputies" that administer controls that include "1. The 'spontaneous' consent given by the great masses of the population to the general direction imposed on social life by dominant fundamental group; this consent is 'historically' caused by the prestige (and consequent confidence) which the dominant

NOTES TO PAGE 17

group enjoys because of its position and function in the world of production. 2. The apparatus of state coercive power which 'legally' enforces discipline on those groups who do not 'consent' either actively or passively. This apparatus, however, is constituted for the whole of society in anticipation of moments of crisis of command and direction when spontaneous consent has failed" ("Intellectuals" 12). *Hegemony*, then, is the phase of "relations of forces" when after ideological confrontation and conflict, one ideology or single combination of ideologies prevails and comes to articulate particular interests as universal. The aims of the dominant are made, more or less by consent of the governed, the aims of society in general. See Gramsci, "The Modern Prince" (181–82).

13. In Gramsci's essential formulation, all people who perform the function of intellectuals emerge from a specific social group or class and are grounded in, tied to, or representative of some social group or class, albeit not necessarily the one from which they emerged. Traditional intellectuals, though they may enjoy a degree of professional autonomy and traverse class boundaries, such as, college professors, basically serve as representatives of the establishment. Organic intellectuals remain connected in some sense to their group of origin and attempt to gain support for the group's ideology or at least some idealized version of it in that group's struggle for power. Gramsci had this distinction in mind:

> The mode of being of the new intellectual can no longer consist in eloquence, which is an exterior and momentary mover of feelings and passions, but in active participation in practical life, as constructor, organizer, "permanent persuader" and not just a simple orator (but superior at the same time to the abstract mathematical spirit); from technique-as-work one proceeds to technique-as-science and to the humanistic conception of history, without which one remains "specialised" and does not become "directive" (specialised and political). Thus there are historically formed specialized categories for the exercise of the intellectual function. They are formed in connection with all social groups, but especially in connection with the more important, and they undergo more extensive and complex elaboration in connection with the dominant social group. One of the most important characteristics of any group that is developing towards dominance is its struggle to assimilate and conquer "ideologically" the traditional intellectuals, but this assimilation and conquest is made quicker and more efficacious the more the group in question succeeds in simultaneously elaborating its own organic intellectuals. ("Intellectuals" 10)

My former student and present colleague Stephen Schneider follows Gramsci more closely than I do and argues strongly that organic intellectuals do not necessarily arise from the groups they represent, that what makes them organic is their commitment to and their role as functionaries for specific groups. He points to—and I appreciate the point—Stokely Carmichael and professional union organizers as examples, the idea being that Carmichael as a child of the Caribbean represented African America and that professional union organizers exhibit solidarity with their constituencies. Schneider's argument makes me reconsider my more restricted read, but I won't back off it yet. Carmichael can be seen and viewed himself as a child of the African diaspora who as a child of the African diaspora expressed a commitment to Pan-Africanism, a diasporic ideology. So a relevant issue is the question of how one defines community of origin. Moreover, the record of professional union organizers is so checkered that it certainly calls into question their function even as representatives. They are not the best examples, collectively, to make a case for solidarity and against the notion of organicism discussed here, though I acknowledge that some case could be made.

14. This phrase is the subtitle of *Prophesy Deliverance!* and (sans the word *an*) the title of the book's concluding chapter.

15. In Taylor Branch's masterful trilogy on America during the King era, one sees plentiful evidence that King certainly knew that African Americans possessed no special gift of nonviolence. For example, Branch describes the scene at the King home in Montgomery after it was bombed: "Little boys dashed around carrying pop bottles broken in half for a fight. Negro men brandished guns and knives, and some confronted the barricade of white policemen shouting for them to disperse" (*Parting the Waters* 165). Branch also discusses King's awareness that the strategy of nonviolent boycott "proved difficult to transplant or expand," and he notes the struggle in Savannah to get local protesters to disarm (*Pillar of Fire* 24, 124–25).

16. See Jerry Watts, *Heroism and the Black Intellectual* (46–52), for discussion of Ellison's political activity in the 1960s. Watts observes, "Ellison is, after all, a meritocratic cultural elitist" (47), held "blatantly antidemocratic views," expressed "distaste for Martin Luther King's criticism of Johnson's war policy" (48), and embraced a politics in which "there was little room for the actively involved, humanistic artist" (49).

17. West's point about Wright's alienation is based in large measure on Wright's emotional distance from the black masses and that he spent the last thirteen years of his life abroad, apparently seeking some sense of home that he could not find in America. But Robeson also spent many years abroad (and might have spent more had not his passport been invalidated during the 1950s) and was not demonstrably closer to the black masses emotionally. Robeson's embrace of black culture finds its analog in Wright's folk history, *12 Million Black Voices*.

18. See, respectively, *Hiphop Literacies*, *Check It While I Wreck It*, and *Race, Rhetoric, and Technology*, 131–37.

3. Socratic Commitment and Critical Literacy

1. For example, Berthoff wrote the foreword and Giroux wrote the introduction to Paulo Freire and Donaldo Macedo's *Literacy*. Ira Shor edited, with Caroline Pari, *Critical Literacy in Action*, which is a tribute to Freire.

2. Original source is Roland Barthes, *Mythologies*, 138.

3. The con position was argued by self-styled conservative Nicholas Stix (see Gilyard and Stix, "Symposium"), who subsequently has attacked me a couple of times in his electronic publications. But a quick surf of the Internet reveals that he has turned his attention to more pressing matters like calling Barry Bonds a racist, defaming Martin Luther King Jr., and railing against what he labels the "gay media mafia."

4. Expanding on his basic idea, Steele theorizes that "endemic devaluation" (68) plagues African American students and that this dynamic, which is culturally systemic, encoded in dominant discourses, and not dependent on strongly prejudiced school officials, can override factors such as money and above-average academic preparation. According to Steele, African American students often face a "jeopardy of double devaluation" (72). In other words, Steele argues, "Like anyone, blacks risk devaluation for a particular incompetence, such as a failed test or a flubbed pronunciation. But they further risk that such performances will confirm the broader, racial inferiority of which they are suspected. Thus, from the first grade through graduate school, blacks have the extra fear that in the eyes of those around them that their full humanity could fall with a poor answer or a mistaken stroke of the pen" (72, 74). Steele's solution, one not only relevant for African American students (nor is his overall conception restricted to the situation of African Americans), is to diminish vulnerability as much as possible and to implement "wise schooling" (75–78), which entails valuing students, challenging them while expecting that they can succeed, eschewing remediation and the accompanying stigma, racial integration, and centralizing African American culture (and other devalued cultures) in the curriculum. At Syracuse, we obviously saw Odyssey as an experiment in wise schooling.

4. Tracking Prophetic Witness

1. Stull reminds us, for example, of King's insistence that "our loyalties must transcend our race, our tribe, our class, and our nation; and this means we must develop a world perspective" and King's argument that "we aren't going to have peace on earth until we recognize this basic fact of the interrelated structure of all reality" (253–54).

2. Stull refers to King's closing: "I still have a dream today that one day war will come to an end, that men will beat their swords into plowshares and their spears into pruning hooks, that nations will no longer rise up against nations, neither will they study war any more. I still have a dream today that one day the lamb and the lion will lie down together and every man will sit under his own vine and fig tree and none shall be afraid. I still have a dream today that one day every valley shall be exalted and every mountain and hill will be made low, the rough places will be made smooth and the crooked places straight, and the glory of the Lord shall be revealed, and all flesh shall see it together. I still have a dream that with this faith we will be able to adjourn the councils of despair and bring new light into the

dark chambers of pessimism. With this faith we will be able to speed up the day when there will be peace on earth and good will toward men. It will be a glorious day, the morning stars will sing together, and the sons of God will shout for joy" (258).

3. In "Transcending Normativity," Wallace rewrites Gere's statement in an attempt to demonstrate how disciplinary discourse in composition could be more inclusive.

> In the academic settings in which I participate, I have noticed that it has become more common and, in some cases, more acceptable to detail the trauma of rape or abuse than to recount a moment of religious inspiration. Indeed, in some academic contexts, it seems now that coming out as a Christian or an observant member of any faith can be as dangerous as making public one's sexual orientation. I don't mean to trivialize rape, physical violence, or the continuing evils of homophobia, heterosexism, and heteronormativity, and I realize that my own Christianity affords me considerable privilege in many contexts of American culture in which LGBT people and those who have suffered sexual and other physical violence continue to face considerable difficulties. Yet I want to argue that there is loss involved when secularizing the American academy—disestablishing the link between higher education and a particular form of Protestant Christianity (which was necessary to open the way for Jews, Catholics, and agnostics in the American academy)—becomes banishing religion altogether in higher education. . . . While my version is admittedly longer, less elegant, and perhaps less provocative than Gere's version, comparing the two suggests four principles that might help us write in ways that are more inclusive of perspectives outside of our own: Resist the urge to imply universality in claims. Ground claims in one's own experiences. Explicitly acknowledge privilege. Attend to the perspective of others. (527)

Although not explicitly connected to composition classrooms, Crowley's *Toward a Civil Discourse*, one of the best books on any subject that I have read in recent years, is indispensable to any discussion of Christian fundamentalism and its relationship to rhetorical education. Crowley points to the hegemonic contest between liberalism and apocalyptism, as well as the often-uncivil nature of it, and proffers the art of rhetoric as a means of productive engagement.

> Since most of the major disagreements that currently circulate in American political discourse arise from conflicts between liberal and apocalyptist approaches to argument, it seems imperative that some means be found that can address their differences. I appeal to rhetoric at this juncture not because I think it is another foundationalism that can solve all disagreements whatsoever. Far from it. But as I have said repeatedly, rhetoric does have a major advantage over liberal strategies

of argument insofar as it is able to address ideological and emotional claims as well as rational ones. I hope to show that well-prepared rhetors can find openings within situations where disagreement occurs, openings that can help participants to conceive of themselves and their relation to events in new ways. To my mind this is at the very least an improvement over the current ideological impasse, to which Americans typically respond with anger or silence. (23)

I view Crowley's project to be outstanding, though I don't necessarily sign on to the claim that "most of the major disagreements" in politics stem from a liberal-apocalyptist clash. For writings on faith and composition beyond those mentioned in this monograph, see Elizabeth Vander Lei and bonnie lenore kyburz's edited collection *Negotiating Religious Faith in the Composition Classroom.*

4. West's words are from "Prophetic Theology," 227.

5. West discusses combative spirituality in "A World of Ideas," 109.

6. *Protopublic* is a term borrowed from my Penn State colleague Rosa A. Eberly. See "From *Writers, Audiences,* and *Communities* to *Publics*: Writing Classrooms as Protopublic Spaces."

7. Marback is right to recognize that the Ebonics debate is only superficially about language and more fundamentally about language attitudes and power relations. Furthermore, he is correct that issues of attitude, power, and democracy should inform public discussions of Ebonics. His primary error lies in equating the "CCCC Statement on Ebonics" with the total response of compositionists in the aftermath of the 1996 resolution in Oakland, California. He continually talks about the inadequacy of "our" reaction and about what "we" need to do. Apparently, he is unaware of the numerous public forums that took place in various communities where some of "us" made the scene. Many of those sessions unfolded pretty much along the lines that he advocates—four or five years after those sessions occurred. An analysis of those types of engagements would have been more beneficial to "us" than a prescription about what some of us publicly active people need to do to go public.

8. Steinberg's essay actually includes a fairly strident critique (33–41) of the concepts that West advances in two essays that appear in *Race Matters,* namely, "Nihilism in Black America" (11–20) and "Beyond Affirmative Action: Equality and Identity" (63–67).

9. For use of the jungle metaphor, see "Nihilism in Black America," 16.

10. Lott expanded his remarks in his recent book *The Disappearing Liberal Intellectual* (111–32). Unfortunately, the latter analysis, though somewhat worthwhile, is marred by a somewhat shrill tone that even turns silly at moments and by Lott's admitted abrasiveness. His logic at times is suspect as well. For example, he insists that "Nihilism in Black America" is a representative text. But what makes it representative in his view is that it has circulated widely, despite that West has spent many more words making

a sharper argument about the relationship between structural oppression and the despair of African Americans. Lott knows this and knows that these other writings are more indicative of the overall nature of West's corpus and thus would be considered by most scholars to be representative texts. But he opts for the criterion of publicity because it's an easier fit for his critique.

11. In a 1976 interview, later included in *Power*, Foucault remarked,

> A new mode of the "connection between theory and practice" has been established. Intellectuals have become used to working not in the modality of the "universal," the "exemplary," the "just-and-true-for-all," but within specific sectors, at the precise points where their own conditions of life or work situate them (housing, the hospital, the asylum, the laboratory, the university, family, and sexual relations). This has undoubtedly given them a more immediate and concrete awareness of struggles. And they have met here with problems that are specific, "nonuniversal," and often different from those of the proletariat or the masses. And yet I believe intellectuals have actually been drawn closer to the proletariat and the masses, for two reasons. First, because it has been a question of real, material, everyday struggles; and second, because they have often been confronted, albeit in a different form, by the same adversary as the proletariat, namely, the multinational corporations, the judicial and police apparatuses, the property speculators, and so on. This is what I would call the "specific" intellectual as opposed to the "universal" intellectual. (126–27)

12. Although my concern here is with the Foucault that West encountered, I surmise that Foucault's latest work, which puts pressure on all of his previous formulations given its stress on subjectivity and is a resource that West has not been privy to, might change a Foucault-West conversation. See, for example, Eric Paras, *Foucault 2.0*, which is based largely on Paras's review of the tapes of twelve semesters of late-career lectures delivered by Foucault at the College of France. As Paras concluded, "Foucault created the twentieth century's most devastating critique of the free subject—and then, in a voice that by the end trembled from pain and debility, liquidated it. For the notion of the end of subjectivity had offered a kind of cold clarity, as well as an immensely thought-provoking lens through which to view the world. But ultimately, only the notion of strong subjectivity proved *warm* enough to accommodate an overwhelming passion for life and an inextinguishable belief in the primacy of human liberty" (158).

5. Tragicomic Hope in Democracy

1. My use of the hyphenated term *spiritual-blues* nods to James Cone's contention in *The Spirituals and the Blues* that the spirituals and the blues are essentially inseparable. As Cone argues, "Unfortunately, it is true that many black church people at first condemned the blues as vulgar and indecent. But that was because they did not understand them rightly. If the blues are

viewed in the proper perspective, it is clear that their mood is very similar to the ethos of the spirituals. Indeed, I contend that the blues and the spirituals flow from the same bedrock of experience, and neither is an adequate interpretation of black life without the commentary of the other" (100).

2. For comments on heteroglossia, the centralizing tendency of dominant discourses, and the functions of the carnival and the official feast, see Mikhail Bakhtin, *The Dialogic Imagination*, 269–73, and *Rabelais and His World*, 4–12.

3. In *Higher Ground* (64–67), Werner provides additional comments about people receiving Mayfield's songs as political inspiration.

4. See West, "Minority Discourse and the Pitfalls of Canon Formation," 200.

5. A. Scott Galloway makes this point in his liner essay that accompanies the twenty-fifth anniversary release of *Superfly*. He argues that the song was "tragically underutilized: "With its mission of outreach to the ghetto young, gifted, and black, imploring them not to be seduced by the 'funky' trappings of 'twinkling twinkling grains,' this anthemic song was likely intended to close the movie, sending filmgoers home with one of Mayfield's patented 'natural highs.' Instead, the chorus is heard only fleetingly in the first song of Curtis' second set back at the club—though you never see him singing it. Its midmovie placement is highly inappropriate thematically, because it plays just after Priest has 'cokes'd' his semiretired mentor, Scatter (played by Julius Harris), into mainlining him thirty keys of dope!""

6. For a sustained treatment of this idea, see Imani Perry, *Prophets of the Hood*, 127–30, 155–90. Central to Perry's argument is the convincing notion that black female rappers have often appropriated the substance of the African American folkloric badman to become female badmen, or "badwomen." Further, she contends, "Hip hop . . . can be credited with the first cultural configuration of the female badman, the badwoman" (167). But to accept the last claim, one has to ignore the bad-women poems of Margaret Walker, especially "Kissie Lee": "Meanest mama you ever seen/She could hold her likker and hold her man/And she went thoo life jus' raisin' san'" (1103).

7. This was written well before Kanye released the CD *Graduation* in September 2007.

8. Bynoe makes a similar argument in *Stand and Deliver*, vii.

9. This is the title of chapter 6, *Democracy Matters*, 174–200.

10. Conversation with Geneva Smitherman, March 24, 2007.

11. In *Word from the Mother*, Geneva Smitherman attributes to Chuck D the comment, "Rap Music is Black folks' CNN" (105). West uses a similar comment from Chuck D—"That's why I call Rap the Black CNN"—as part of an epigraph for chapter 6, *Democracy Matters*, 174. In *Fight the Power*, Chuck D remarks, "When Public Enemy first came out we used to say, 'Public Enemy, we're agents for the preservation of the Black mind. We're media hijackers.' We worked to hijack the media and put it in our own form. That's originally how we came out. Initially Rap was America's informal CNN because when Rap records came out somebody from far away could

listen to a Rap record because it uses so many descriptive words and get a visual picture from what was being said. So a person that was coming up in Oakland would listen to a record from New York and get a visualization of what New York was about. When rappers came out of Oakland and Los Angeles and they were very visual with their words, people all over could get informed about Black life in those areas without checking the news. Every time we checked for ourselves on the news they were locking us up anyway, so the interpretation coming from Rap was a lot clearer. That's why I call Rap the Black CNN" (256).

6. Landing Song

1. Friedrich Nietzsche, *Thus Spoke Zarathustra*, 152–53.

2. The relevant passage from *Ars Poetica*—"*Aut prodesse volunt, aut delectare poetae*"—has been translated numerous ways. Dunsany and Oakley's translation—"A poet should instruct, or please, or both"—is close to West's interpretation (Horace 43).

3. Flower's work is mentioned earlier in the text, most notably in chapter 3. For an example of Royer and Gilles's project, see "Directed Self-Placement: An Attitude of Orientation."

4. See West's foreword, 11–15.

5. Of the various translations of Leopardi's line from "L'Infinito"—"*e il naufragar m'e dulce in questo mare*"—Paul Lawton comes closest to the idea of the "mind's sweet shipwreck." He translates, "and sweet it is to shipwreck in this sea" (Leopardi 55).

6. West is referring partly to Glaude's recent project of demonstrating Dewey's relevance to contemporary African American politics. See Glaude, *In a Shade of Blue: Pragmatism and the Politics of Black America*.

7. Horton further explained, "The reason it was such a debatable subject is because the overwhelming majority of the people who were organizing and who were officials of unions in the South had been at Highlander. So the public who only saw that didn't know what went on at Highlander, and they assumed that we were an organizer's training school. But I kept saying no, no. We do education and they become organized. They become officials. They become whatever they are, educational directors. Basically it's not technical training. We're not in the technical business. We emphasize ways you analyze and perform and relate to people, but that's what I call education, not organizing. When I wanted to organize—which I did at one period, something I'll go into later on—I resigned from the Highlander staff. I took a leave of absence from the Highlander staff because I didn't want organizing and education confused in the minds of the people. It was confusing enough as it was" (115–16).

8. I make no attempt to document every allusion made, an idea that is impractical given the nature of the interview. But I can identify Ransby's book, *Ella Baker and the Black Freedom Movement*.

9. I am referring to Wolin's *Berkeley Rebellion and Beyond*.

Bibliography

Alim, H. Samy. *Roc the Mic Right: The Language of Hip Hop Culture*. New York: Routledge, 2006.

————. *You Know My Steez: An Ethnographic and Sociolinguistic Study of Style-shifting in a Black American Speech Community*. Durham: Duke University Press, 2005.

Alinsky, Saul D. *Reveille for Radicals*. 1946. Reprint, New York: Vintage, 1989.

————. *Rules for Radicals: A Pragmatic Primer for Realistic Radicals*. New York: Random House, 1971.

Allen, Theodore. *The Invention of the White Race, Volume 1: Racial Oppression and Social Control*. New York: Verso, 1994.

Bakhtin, Mikhail. *The Dialogic Imagination: Four Essays*. Edited by Michael Holquist. Translated by Caryl Emerson and Michael Holquist. Austin: University of Texas Press, 1981.

————. *Rabelais and His World*. Translated by Helene Iswolsky. Bloomington: Indiana University Press, 1984.

Ball, Arnetha F., and Ted Lardner. *African American Literacies Unleashed: Vernacular English and the Composition Classroom*. Carbondale: Southern Illinois University Press, 2005.

Banks, Adam J. *Race, Rhetoric, and Technology: Searching for Higher Ground*. Mahwah, NJ: Erlbaum, 2006.

Barthes, Roland. *Mythologies*. Translated by Annette Lavers. New York: Hill and Wang, 1972.

Beech, Jennifer. "Redneck and Hillbilly Discourse in the Writing Classroom: Classifying Critical Pedagogies of Whiteness." *College English* 67 (2004): 172–86.

Bego, Mark. *Aretha Franklin: The Queen of Soul*. Cambridge, MA: Da Capo/Perseus, 2001.

Berlin, James A. *Rhetorics, Poetics, and Cultures: Refiguring College English Studies*. Urbana, IL: National Council of Teachers of English, 1996.

Bernstein, Eduard. *Evolutionary Socialism: The Classic Statement of Democratic Socialism*. New York: Schocken, 1965.

Berthoff, Ann. Foreword. In *Literacy: Reading the Word and the World*. By Paulo Freire and Donaldo Macedo. New York: Bergin, 1987. xi–xxiii.

Bitzer, Lloyd. "The Rhetorical Situation." *Philosophy and Rhetoric* 1 (1968): 1–14.

Bizzell, Patricia. "William Perry and Liberal Education." *College English* 46 (1984): 447–54.

Blackman, Toni. "The Feminine Voice in Hip Hop." *Inner-Course: A Plea for Real Love*. New York: Villard, 2003. 100–102.

Branch, Taylor. *Parting the Waters: America in the King Years, 1954–1963*. New York: Simon & Schuster, 1989.

———. *Pillar of Fire: America in the King Years, 1963–1965*. New York: Simon & Schuster, 1998.

Brown, Claude. "The Language of Soul." *Esquire*, April 1968, 88, 160–61.

Burns, Peter. *Curtis Mayfield: People Never Give Up*. London: Sanctuary House, 2003.

Bynoe, Yvonne. *Stand and Deliver: Political Activism, Leadership, and Hip Hop Culture*. New York: Soft Skull, 2004.

Chuck D., with Yusuf Jah. *Fight the Power: Rap, Race, and Reality*. New York: Dell, 1997.

Clark, Romy, and Roz Ivanič. *The Politics of Writing*. London: Routledge, 1997.

Common. *Be*. CD. Geffen Records, 2005.

Cone, James H. 1972. *The Spirituals and the Blues: An Interpretation*. Reprint, Maryknoll, NY: Orbis, 1992.

Conway, Jill Kerr. *The Road from Coorain*. New York: Knopf, 1989.

Corredor, Eva. "On the Influence of Lukacs: Interview with Cornel West." In *Beyond Eurocentrism and Multiculturalism. Volume 2, Prophetic Reflections; Notes on Race and Power in America*. Monroe, ME: Common Courage, 1993. 47–71.

Cowan, Rosemary. *Cornel West: The Politics of Redemption*. Cambridge: Polity, 2003.

Crawford, Ilene. "Building a Theory of Affect in Cultural Studies Composition Pedagogy." *JAC* 22 (2002): 678–84.

Crowley, Sharon. *Toward a Civil Discourse: Rhetoric and Fundamentalism*. Pittsburgh: University of Pittsburgh Press, 2006.

Daniell, Beth. "Narratives of Literacy: Connecting Composition to Culture." *College Composition and Communication* 50 (1999): 393–410.

Dead Prez. *It's Bigger Than Hip-Hop*. TV. Directed by John Threat. Starz Entertainment Group, 2006.

———. *Let's Get Free*. CD. Loud Records, 2000.

———. *Revolutionary but Gangsta*. CD. Sony Music Entertainment, 2004.

Destigter, Todd. "Good Deeds: An Ethnographer's Reflections on Useful-
ness." In *Literacy and Democracy: Teacher Research and Composition
Studies in Pursuit of Habitable Spaces*. Edited by Cathy Fleischer and
David Schaafsma. Urbana, IL: National Council of Teachers of English,
1998. 28–52.

———. *Reflections of a Teacher Citizen*. Urbana, IL: National Council of
Teachers of English, 2001.

Dewey, John. "The Development of American Pragmatism." In *The Philoso-
phy of John Dewey*. Edited by John J. McDermott. Chicago: University of
Chicago Press, 1981. Quoted in Cornel West, *Cornel West Reader*, New
York: Basic *Civitas*, 1999.

Dillard, Annie. *An American Childhood*. New York: Perennial Library,
1988.

Dobard, Raymond G., and Jacquelin L. Tobin. *Hidden in Plain View: A Secret Story of Quilts and the Underground Railroad*. New York: Anchor,
2000.

Dobkin, Matt. *I Never Loved a Man the Way I Love You: Aretha Franklin,
Respect, and the Making of a Soul Music Masterpiece*. New York: St.
Martin's, 2004.

Du Bois, W. E. B. *The Souls of Black Folk*. 1903. Reprint, New York: Penguin,
1989.

Dunbar, Paul Laurence. "An Ante-Bellum Sermon." In *The Black Poets*.
Edited by Dudley Randall. New York: Bantam, 1971. 44–46.

Durst, Russell K. *Collision Course: Conflict, Negotiation, and Learning in
College Composition*. Urbana, IL: National Council of Teachers of
English, 1999.

Dyson, Michael Eric. *Mercy, Mercy Me: The Art, Loves and Demons of Marvin
Gaye*. New York: Basic *Civitas*, 2005.

Eberly, Rosa A. "From *Writers, Audiences,* and *Communities* to *Publics*:
Writing Classrooms as Protopublic Spaces." *Rhetoric Review* 18 (1999):
165–78.

Edmonds, Ben. *What's Going On? Marvin Gaye and the Last Days of the
Motown Sound*. Edinburgh: Canongate, 2002.

Ehrenreich, Barbara. "What I've Learned from Men." In *Rhetorical Choices:
A Reader for Writers*. Edited by Keith Gilyard, Deborah H. Holdstein,
and Charles I. Schuster. New York: Pearson Longman, 2004. 258–61.

Fishman, Andrea. *Amish Literacy: What It Means and How*. Portsmouth,
NH: Heinemann, 1988.

Fishman, Stephen M., and Lucille McCarthy. *John Dewey and the Challenge
of Classroom Practice*. New York: Teachers College Press, 1998.

———. *Whose Goals Whose Aspirations: Learning to Teach Underprepared
Writers Across the Curriculum*. Logan: Utah State University Press,
2002.

Fleckenstein, Kristie S. "Bodysigns: A Biorhetoric for Change." *JAC* 21
(2001): 761-90.

Flower, Linda. "An Experimental Way of Knowing." In *Learning to Rival: A Literate Practice for Intercultural Inquiry.* Mahwah, NJ: Lawrence Erlbaum, 2000. 49–80.

———. "The Rival Hypothesis Stance and the Practice of Inquiry." In *Learning to Rival: A Literate Practice for Intercultural Inquiry.* Mahwah, NJ: Lawrence Erlbaum, 2000. 27–47.

———. "Talking across Difference: Intercultural Rhetoric and the Search for Situated Knowledge." *College Composition and Communication* 55 (2003): 38–68.

Flower, Linda, Elenore Long, and Lorraine Higgins. *Learning to Rival: A Literate Practice for Intercultural Inquiry.* Mahwah, NJ: Lawrence Erlbaum, 2000.

Foucault, Michel. *The Archaeology of Knowledge and the Discourse on Language.* Translated by A. M. Sheridan Smith. 1969. Reprint, New York: Pantheon, 1972.

———. *Discipline and Punish: The Birth of the Prison.* Translated by Alan Sheridan. 1975. Reprint, New York: Vintage, 1995.

———. *Fearless Speech.* Edited by Joseph Pearson. Los Angeles: Semiotext(e), 2001.

———. *The History of Sexuality: An Introduction, Volume 1.* 1976. Translated by Robert Hurley. Reprint, New York: Vintage, 1990.

———. *Language, Counter-Memory, Practice: Selected Essays and Interviews by Michel Foucault.* Edited by Donald F. Bouchard. Translated by Donald F. Bouchard and Sherry Simon. Ithaca, NY: Cornell University Press, 1980.

———. *Madness and Civilization: A History of Insanity in the Age of Reason.* Translated by Richard Howard. 1961. Reprint, New York: Vintage, 1988.

———. *The Order of Things: An Archaeology of the Human Sciences.* 1966. New York: Vintage, 1994.

———. *Power.* Edited by James D. Faubion. Translated by Robert Hurley and others. New York: New Press, 1994.

———. *Power/Knowledge: Selected Interviews and Other Writings, 1972–1977.* Edited by Colin Gordon. Translated by Colin Gordon, Leo Marshall, John Mepham, and Kate Soper. New York: Pantheon, 1980.

Fox, Tom. *Defending Access: A Critique of Standards in Higher Education.* Portsmouth, NH: Boynton/Cook, 1999.

———. "Race and Collective Resistance." In *Insurrections: Approaches to Resistance in Composition Studies.* Edited by Andrea Greenbaum. Albany: State University of New York Press, 2001. 71–86.

Franklin, Aretha. *The Delta Meets Detroit: Aretha's Blues.* CD. Atlantic Recording, 1998.

———. *The Very Best of Aretha Franklin: The '60s.* CD. Atlantic Recording, 1994.

Franklin, Aretha, and David Ritz. *From These Roots.* New York: Villard, 1999.

Freire, Paulo. *Pedagogy of the Oppressed*. Translated by Myra Bergman Ramos. New York: Continuum, 1970.

Freire, Paulo, and Donaldo Macedo. *Literacy: Reading the Word and the World*. New York: Bergin & Garvey, 1987.

Galloway, A. Scott. "Liner Notes." *Superfly*. CD. Rhino Entertainment, 1997.

Gaye, Marvin. *What's Going On*. CD. Tamla, 2002.

Gilyard, Keith. "African American Contributions to Composition Studies." *College Composition and Communication* 50 (1999): 626–44.

———. "Basic Writing, Cost Effectiveness, and Ideology." *Journal of Basic Writing* 19 (2000): 36–42.

———. *Voices of the Self: A Study of Language Competence*. Detroit: Wayne State University Press, 1991.

Gilyard, Keith, and Elaine Richardson. "Students' Right to Possibility: Basic Writing and African American Rhetoric." In *Insurrections: Approaches to Resistance in Composition Studies*. Edited by Andrea Greenbaum. Albany: State University of New York Press, 2001. 37–51.

Gilyard, Keith, Nance Hahn, and Faith Plvan. *The Odyssey Project: Readings for Writing 105*. Dubuque, IA: Kendall/Hunt, 1997.

Gilyard, Keith, and Nicholas Stix. "Symposium: Would Ebonics Programs in Public Schools Be a Good Idea?" *Washington Times Insight on the News*, March 31, 1997.

Giroux, Henry. Introduction. In *Literacy: Reading the Word and the World*. By Paulo Freire and Donaldo Macedo. New York: Bergin & Garvey, 1987. 1–27.

Giroux, Henry, and Susan Searls Giroux. *Take Back Higher Education: Race, Youth, and the Crisis of Democracy in the Post–Civil Rights Era*. New York: Palgrave, 2004.

Glaude, Eddie S., Jr. *In a Shade of Blue: Pragmatism and the Politics of Black America*. Chicago: University of Chicago Press, 2007.

Goodburn, Amy. "It's a Question of Faith: Discourses of Fundamentalism and Critical Pedagogy in the Writing Classroom." *JAC* 18 (1998): 333–53.

Gramsci, Antonio. "The Intellectuals." In *Selections from the Prison Notebooks of Antonio Gramsci*. Edited and translated by Quintin Hoare and Geoffrey Nowell Smith. New York: International, 1971. 3–23.

———. "The Modern Prince." In *Selections from the Prison Notebooks of Antonio Gramsci*. Edited and translated by Quintin Hoare and Geoffrey Nowell Smith. New York: International, 1971. 123–205.

———. *Selections from the Prison Notebooks of Antonio Gramsci*. Edited and translated by Quintin Hoare and Geoffrey Nowell Smith. New York: International, 1971.

———. "Workers' Democracy." In *The Antonio Gramsci Reader: Selected Writings, 1916–1935*. Edited by David Forgacs. New York: New York University Press, 2000. 79–82.

Guinier, Lani. "The Tyranny of the Majority." In *Rhetorical Choices: A Reader for Writers*. Edited by Keith Gilyard, Deborah H. Holdstein, and Charles I. Schuster. New York: Pearson Longman, 2004. 607–12.

Heilker, Paul. *The Essay: Theory and Pedagogy for an Active Form*. Urbana, IL: National Council of Teachers of English, 1996.

Hesford, Wendy. *Framing Identities: Autobiography and the Politics of Pedagogy*. Minneapolis: University of Minnesota Press, 1999.

Hobbes, Thomas. *Leviathan*. 1651. Reprint, New York: Penguin Classics, 1985.

Holmes, David G. *Revisiting Racialized Voice: African American Ethos in Language and Literature*. Carbondale: Southern Illinois University Press, 2004.

hooks, bell. *Teaching Community: A Pedagogy of Hope*. New York: Routledge, 2003.

———. *Teaching to Transgress: Education as the Practice of Freedom*. New York: Routledge, 1994.

Horace. "The Art of Poetry." In *The Complete Works of Horace*. Translated by Lord Dunsany and Michael Oakley. London: Dent & Sons, 1911. 133–47.

Horton, Myles, and Paulo Freire. *We Make the Road by Walking: Conversations on Education and Social Change*. Edited by Brenda Bell, John Gaventa, and John Peters. Philadelphia: Temple University Press, 1990.

Hughes, Langston. "Theme for English B." In *The Collected Poems of Langston Hughes*. Edited by Arnold Rampersad. New York: Vintage, 1994. 409–10.

Hurlbert, Claude, Derek Owens, and Robert Yagelski. "Making 4Cs Matter More." *Writing on the Edge* 15 (2005): 67–91.

Immortal Technique. *Revolutionary Vol. 1*. CD. Viper Records, 2001.

———. *Revolutionary Vol. 2*. CD. Viper Records, 2003.

Interchanges. "Spiritual Sites of Composing." *College Composition and Communication* 45 (1994): 237–63.

Jackson, Ronald L., II. "Afrocentricity as Metatheory: A Dialogic Exploration of Its Principles." In *Understanding African American Rhetoric: Classical Origins to Contemporary Innovations*. Edited by Ronald L. Jackson II and Elaine Richardson. New York: Routledge, 2003. 115–29.

———. "Exploring African American Identity Negotiation in the Academy: Toward a Transformative Vision of African American Communication Scholarship." *Howard Journal of Communications* 13 (2002): 43–57.

Jackson, Shirley. "A Fine Old Firm." In *The Lottery and Other Stories*. New York: Farrar, Strauss, and Giroux, 1982. 193–97.

James, William. *Pragmatism: A New Name for Some Old Ways of Thinking*. 1907. Reprint, New York: Barnes & Noble, 2003.

Jean Grae. *The Attack of the Attacking Things: The Dirty Mixes*. CD. Third Earth Music, 2002.

———. *This Week*. CD. Babygrande Records, 2004.

Johnson, Clarence Shole. *Cornel West and Philosophy: The Quest for Social Justice*. New York: Routledge, 2003.

Kanae, Lisa. "Pidgin." *Rhetorical Choices: A Reader for Writers*. Edited by Keith Gilyard, Deborah H. Holdstein, and Charles I. Schuster. New York: Pearson Longman, 2004. 146–62.

Kates, Susan. "The Embodied Rhetoric of Hallie Quinn Brown." *College English* 59 (1997): 59–71.

Kells, Michelle Hall. *Hector P. Garcia: Everyday Rhetoric and Mexican American Civil Rights*. Carbondale: Southern Illinois University Press, 2006.

Kells, Michelle Hall, Valerie Balester, and Victor Villanueva, eds. *Latino/a Discourses: On Language, Identity and Literacy Education*. Portsmouth, NH: Boynton/Cook, 1997.

Kincaid, Jamaica. "Girl." In *Rhetorical Choices: A Reader for Writers*. Edited by Keith Gilyard, Deborah H. Holdstein, and Charles I. Schuster. New York: Pearson Longman, 2004. 136–37.

King, Martin Luther, Jr. "A Christmas Sermon on Peace." In *A Testament of Hope: The Essential Writings and Speeches of Martin Luther King Jr.* Edited by James Melvin Washington. San Francisco: HarperSanFrancisco, 1991. 253–58.

———. "Letter from Birmingham City Jail." In *A Testament of Hope: The Essential Writings and Speeches of Martin Luther King Jr.* Edited by James Melvin Washington. San Francisco: HarperSanFrancisco, 1991. 289–302.

Kopelson, Karen. "Rhetoric on the Edge of Cunning; Or, the Performance of Neutrality (Re)Considered as a Composition Pedagogy for Student Resistance." *College Composition and Communication* 55 (2003): 115–46.

Korsch, Karl. "Fundamentals of Socialization." 1919. In *Karl Korsch: Revolutionary Theory*. Edited by Douglas Kellner. Austin: University of Texas Press, 1977. 124–33.

Kutz, Eleanor, and Hepzibah Roskelly. *An Unquiet Pedagogy*. Portsmouth, NH: Boynton/Cook, 1991.

Kweli, Talib. *Quality*. CD. Rawkus Entertainment, 2002.

———. *Right About Now*. CD. Koch Records, 2005.

Kweli, Talib, and Hi-Tek. *Reflection Eternal*. CD. Rawkus Entertainment, 2000.

Kynard, Carmen. "'Trying to Bend the Tree When It Is Already Grown': Spanning the Spectrum of African Diaspora Englishes in the College Writing Classroom." In *Teaching English Today: Advocating Change in the Secondary Curriculum*. Edited by Barrie R. C. Barrell, Roberta F. Hammett, John S. Mayher, and Gordon M. Pradl. New York: Teachers College Press, 2004. 92–105.

Lakoff, Robin Tolmach. *The Language War*. Berkeley: University of California Press, 2001.

Lazere, Donald. "Teaching the Political Conflicts: *A Rhetorical Schema*." In *Critical Literacy in Action: Writing Words, Changing Worlds*. Edited by Ira Shor and Caroline Pari. Portsmouth, NH: Boynton/Cook, 1999. 258–79.

Lei, Elizabeth Vander, and bonnie lenore kyburz. *Negotiating Religious Faith in the Composition Classroom*. Portsmouth, NH: Boynton/Cook, 2005.

Lenin, Vladimir. *One Step Forward, Two Steps Back*. 1903. Reprint, New York: Pathfinder, 1999.

———. *What Is to Be Done?* 1902. In *Essential Works of Lenin*. Reprint, Mineola, NY: Dover, 1987. 53–176.

Leopardi, Giacomo. "The Infinite." In *Canti*. Edited by Franco Fortino. Translated by Paul Lawton. Dublin: UCD Foundation for Italian Studies, 1996. 55.

Levinson, Stephen C. *Pragmatics*. Cambridge: Cambridge University Press, 1983.

Lindquist, Julie. "Class Affects, Classroom Affectations: Working through the Paradoxes of Strategic Empathy." *College English* 67 (2004): 187–209.

Linkon, Sherry Lee, Irvin Peckham, and Benjamin G. Lanier-Nabors. "Struggling with Class in English Studies." *College English* 67 (2004): 149–53.

Lopate, Phillip. Introduction. In *The Art of the Personal Essay: An Anthology from the Classical Era to the Present*. Edited by Phillip Lopate. New York: Anchor, 1995. xxxiii–liv.

Lott, Eric. "Cornel West in the Hour of Chaos: Culture and Politics in Race Matters." *Social Text* 40 (1994): 39–50.

———. *The Disappearing Liberal Intellectual*. New York: Basic, 2006.

Lu, Min-Zhan. "An Essay on the Work of Composition: Composing English against the Order of Fast Capitalism." *College Composition and Communication* 56 (2004): 16–50.

———. "Professing Multiculturalism: The Politics of Style in the Contact Zone." *College Composition and Communication* 45 (1994): 442–58.

———. "Redefining the Literate Self: The Politics of Critical Affirmation." *College Composition and Communication* 51 (1999): 172–94.

Luxemburg, Rosa. "Organizational Questions of Russian Social Democracy." 1904. In *The Rosa Luxemburg Reader*. Edited by Peter Hudis and Kevin B. Anderson. New York: Monthly Review, 2004. 248–65.

———. "Social Reform or Revolution." 1899. In *The Rosa Luxemburg Reader*. Edited by Peter Hudis and Kevin B. Anderson. New York: Monthly Review, 2004. 128–67.

Mailloux, Steven. *Reception Histories: Rhetoric, Pragmatism, and American Cultural Politics*. Ithaca, NY: Cornell University Press, 1998.

Marable, Manning. "The Politics of Hip Hop." *Along the Color Line*, March 2002. http://www.hartford-hwp.com/archives/45a/594.html 1–4.

Marback, Richard. "From Athens to Detroit: Civic Space and Learning Writing." *Rhetoric Review* 15 (1996): 156–73.

———. "Corbett's Hand: A Rhetorical Figure for Composition Studies." *College Composition and Communication* 47 (1996): 180–98.

———. "Detroit and the Closed Fist: Toward a Theory of Material Rhetoric." *Rhetoric Review* 17 (1998): 74–92.

———. "Ebonics: Theorizing in Public Our Attitudes toward Literacy." *College Composition and Communication* 53 (2001): 11–32.

———. "Police Violence and Denials of Race." In *Rhetoric and Ethnicity*. Edited by Keith Gilyard and Vorris Nunley. Portsmouth, NH: Boynton/Cook, 2004. 77–84.

Marcuse, Herbert. *An Essay on Liberation*. Boston: Beacon, 1969.

Marx, Karl. *Capital: A Critique of Political Economy, Volume 1*. 1867. Translated by Ben Fowkes. Reprint, New York: Penguin Classics, 1990.

———. *The Portable Karl Marx*. Edited by Eugene Kamenka. New York: Viking Penguin, 1983.

Marx, Karl, and Frederick Engels. *The Communist Manifesto*. 1848. Reprint, London: Verso, 1998.

———. *The German Ideology, Part One with Selections from Parts Two and Three and Supplementary Texts*. Edited by C. J. Arthur. New York: International, 1970.

Matthews, Victoria Earle. "The Value of Race Literature: An Address Delivered at the First Congress of Colored Women of the United States." In *With Pen and Voice: A Critical Anthology of Nineteenth-Century African-American Women*. Edited by Shirley Wilson Logan. Carbondale: Southern Illinois University Press, 1995. 126–48.

Mayfield, Curtis. *Curtis Mayfield and the Impressions: The Anthology, 1961–1977*. CD. MCA Records, 1992.

McChesney, Robert, and John Nichols. *Our Media, Not Theirs: The Democratic Struggle against Corporate Media*. New York: Seven Stories, 2002.

McClaren, Peter L., and Michael Dantley. "Leadership and a Critical Pedagogy of Race: Cornel West, Stuart Hall, and the Prophetic Tradition." *Journal of Negro Education* 59 (1990): 29–44.

McCrary, Donald. "Womanist Theology and Its Efficacy for the Writing Classroom." *College Composition and Communication* 52 (2001): 521–52.

Miller, Keith D. "City Called Freedom: Biblical Metaphor in Spirituals, Gospel Lyrics, and the Civil Rights Movement." In *African Americans and the Bible: Sacred Texts and Social Textures*. Edited by Vincent L. Wimbush. New York: Continuum, 2000. 546–55.

Miller, Richard E. "The Nervous System." *College English* 58 (1996): 265–86.

Morgan, Marcyliena. *Language, Discourse and Power in African American Culture*. Cambridge: Cambridge University Press, 2002.

Morrison, Toni. *The Bluest Eye*. New York: Washington Square, 1970.

Mukherjee, Bharati. "Two Ways to Belong in America." In *Rhetorical Choices: A Reader for Writers*. Edited by Keith Gilyard, Deborah H. Holdstein, and Charles I. Schuster. New York: Pearson Longman, 2004. 413–16.

Mutnick, Deborah. *Writing in an Alien World: Basic Writing and the Struggle for Equality in Higher Education*. Portsmouth, NH: Boynton/Cook, 1996.

Nietzsche, Friedrich. *Thus Spoke Zarathustra*. In *The Portable Nietzsche*. Edited and translated by Walter Kaufmann. New York: Penguin, 1982. 103–439.

Ohmann, Richard. *English in America: A Radical View of the Profession*. 1976. Reprint, Hanover, NH: Wesleyan University Press, 1996.

Okawa, Gail Y. "Removing Masks: Confronting Graceful Evasion and Bad Habits in a Graduate English Class." In *Race, Rhetoric, and Composition*. Edited by Keith Gilyard. Portsmouth, NH: Boynton/Cook, 1999. 124–43.

Olney, James. *Metaphors of Self: The Meaning of Autobiography*. Princeton, NJ: Princeton University Press, 1972.

Paglia, Camille. "It's a Jungle Out There." In *Rhetorical Choices: A Reader for Writers*. Edited by Keith Gilyard, Deborah H. Holdstein, and Charles I. Schuster. New York: Pearson Longman, 2004. 602–6.

Pannekoek, Anton. "Marxist Theory and Revolutionary Tactics." 1912. In *Pannekoek and Gorter's Marxism*. Edited by D. A. Smart. London: Pluto Press, 1978. 50–73.

Paras, Eric. *Foucault 2.0: Beyond Power and Knowledge*. New York: Other, 2006.

Parks, Stephen. *Class Politics: The Movement for the Students' Right to Their Own Language*. Urbana, IL: National Council of Teachers of English, 2000.

Payne, Charles M., Jr. *I've Got the Light of Freedom: The Organizing Tradition and the Mississippi Freedom Struggle*. 1995. Reprint, Berkeley: University of California Press, 1997.

Perkins, Priscilla. "'A Radical Conversion of the Mind': Fundamentalism, Hermeneutics, and the Metanoic Classroom." *College English* 63 (2001): 585–611.

Perry, Imani. *Prophets of the Hood: Politics and Poetics in Hip Hop*. Durham, NC: Duke University Press, 2004.

Perry, Theresa, and Lisa Delpit, eds. *The Real Ebonics Debate: Power, Language, and the Education of African-American Children*. Boston: Beacon, 1998.

Perry, William C., Jr. *Forms of Intellectual and Ethical Development in the College Years: A Scheme*. New York: Holt, Rinehart, and Winston, 1968.

Plato. *Apology*. Translated by Hugh Tredennick. *The Collected Dialogues of Plato including the Letters*. Edited by Edith Hamilton and Huntington Cairns. Princeton, NJ: Princeton University Press, 1989. 3–26.

———. *Meno.* Translated by W. K. C. Guthrie. *The Collected Dialogues of Plato including the Letters.* Edited by Edith Hamilton and Huntington Cairns. Princeton, NJ: Princeton University Press, 1989. 353–84.

———. *Phaedrus.* Translated by R. Hackforth. *The Collected Dialogues of Plato including the Letters.* Edited by Edith Hamilton and Huntington Cairns. Princeton, NJ: Princeton University Press, 1989. 475–525.

Plvan, Faith. "The Odyssey Project: Conception, Initiation, Modification: Initiating the Project." Panel presentation, annual convention of the Conference on College Composition and Communication, San Diego, CA, April 2, 1993.

Poovey, Mary. "Cultural Criticism: Past and Present." *College English* 52 (1990): 615–25.

Pough, Gwendolyn. *Check It While I Wreck It: Black Womanhood, Hip-Hop Culture, and the Public Sphere.* Boston: Northeastern University Press, 2004.

Pradl, Gordon M. *Literature for Democracy: Reading as a Social Act.* Portsmouth, NH: Boynton/Cook, 1996.

Pruter, Robert. Liner notes. *Curtis Mayfield and the Impressions: The Anthology, 1961–1977.* CD. MCA Records, 1992.

Rabinow, Paul, ed. *The Foucault Reader.* New York: Pantheon, 1984.

Rabinow, Paul, and Nikolas Rose, eds. *The Essential Foucault: Selections from Essential Works of Foucault, 1954–1984.* New York: New Press, 2003.

Rand, Lizabeth A. "Enacting Faith: Evangelical Discourse and the Discipline of Composition Studies." *College Composition and Communication* 52 (2001): 349–67.

Ransby, Barbara. *Ella Baker and the Black Freedom Movement: A Radical Democratic Vision.* Chapel Hill: University of North Carolina Press, 2002.

Ratcliffe, Krista. "Rhetorical Listening: A Trope for Interpretive Invention and a 'Code of Cross-Cultural Conduct.'" *College Composition and Communication* 51 (1999): 195–224.

Richardson, Elaine. *African American Literacies.* New York: Routledge, 2003.

———. *Hiphop Literacies.* New York: Routledge, 2006.

Rickford, John Russell, and Russell John Rickford. *Spoken Soul: The Story of Black English.* New York: John Wiley & Sons, 2000.

Ritz, David. *Divided Soul: The Life of Marvin Gaye.* Cambridge, MA: Da Capo/Perseus, 1991.

Rodriguez, Richard. *Hunger of Memory: The Education of Richard Rodriguez.* New York: Bantam, 1983.

Ronald, Kate, and Hephzibah Roskelly. "Untested Feasibility: Imagining the Pragmatic Possibility of Paulo Freire." *College English* 63 (2001): 612–32.

Rorty, Richard. *Achieving Our Country: Leftist Thought in Twentieth-Century America.* Cambridge, MA: Harvard University Press, 1998.

————. "Anticlericalism and Atheism." In Rorty and Vattimo, *The Future of Religion*, 29–41.

Rorty, Richard, and Gianni Vattimo. *The Future of Religion*. Edited by Santiago Zabala. New York: Columbia University Press, 2005.

Rose, Mike. *Lives on the Boundary: The Struggles and Achievements of America's Underprepared*. New York: Free Press, 1989.

Rosenblatt, Louise. *The Reader, the Text, the Poem: The Transactional Theory of the Literary Work*. 1978. Reprint, Carbondale: Southern Illinois University Press, 1994.

Roskelly, Hephzibah, and Kate Ronald. *Reason to Believe: Romanticism, Pragmatism, and the Teaching of Writing*. Albany: State University of New York Press, 1998.

Rousseau, Jean-Jacques. "Discourse on the Origin and Foundations of Inequality among Men." 1755. In *Rousseau's Political Writings*. Edited by Alan Ritter and Julia Conaway Bondanella. Translated by Julia Conaway Bondanella. New York: Norton, 1988. 3–57.

Royer, Daniel J., and Roger Gilles. "Directed Self-Placement: An Attitude of Orientation." *College Composition and Communication* 50 (1998): 54–70.

Royster, Jacqueline Jones. "When the First Voice You Hear Is Not Your Own." *College Composition and Communication* 47 (1996): 29–40.

Russell, Bertrand. *A History of Western Philosophy*. New York: Simon & Schuster, 1945.

Sanjek, Roger. "The Enduring Inequalities of Race." In *Race*. Edited by Steven Gregory and Roger Sanjek. New Brunswick, NJ: Rutgers University Press. 1–17.

Seitz, David. "Making Work Visible." *College English* 67 (2004): 210–21.

Selsam, Harry. "Marxism versus Pragmatism." *Masses and Mainstream*, May 1954, 61–64.

Severino, Carol. "Two Approaches to 'Cultural Text': Toward Multicultural Literacy." In *Writing in Multicultural Settings*. Edited by Carol Severino, Juan Guerra, and Johnnella Butler. New York: Modern Language Association, 1997. 106–17.

Shor, Ira. "What Is Literacy?" In *Critical Literacy in Action: Writing Words, Changing Worlds*. Edited by Ira Shor and Caroline Pari. Portsmouth, NH: Boynton/Cook, 1999. 1–30.

Shor, Ira, and Caroline Pari. *Critical Literacy in Action: Writing Words, Changing Worlds*. Portsmouth, NH: Boynton/Cook, 1999.

Smitherman, Geneva. *Talkin and Testifyin: The Language of Black America*. Boston: Houghton Mifflin, 1977.

————. *Talkin That Talk: Language, Culture, and Education in African America*. New York: Routledge, 2000.

————. *Word from the Mother: Language and African Americans*. New York: Routledge, 2006.

Soliday, Mary. "Translating Self and Difference through Literacy Narratives." *College English* 56 (1994): 511–26.

Stalin, Joseph. *Concerning Questions of Leninism*. In *Works*. Volume 8. Moscow: Foreign Languages Publishing House, 1954. 13–96.

———. *The Foundations of Leninism: Lectures Delivered at the Sverdlov University*. In *Works*. Volume 6. Moscow: Foreign Language Publishing House, 1953. 71–196.

Stampp, Kenneth M. "To Make Them Stand in Fear." In *Rhetorical Choices: A Reader for Writers*. Edited by Keith Gilyard, Deborah H. Holdstein, and Charles I. Schuster. New York: Pearson Longman, 2004. 361–64.

Steele, Claude M. "Race and the Schooling of Black Americans." *Atlantic Monthly*, April 1992, 68–78.

Steinberg, Michael P. *Listening to Reason: Culture, Subjectivity, and Nineteenth-Century Music*. Princeton, NJ: Princeton University Press, 2004.

Steinberg, Stephen. "The Liberal Retreat from Race during the Post–Civil Rights Era." In *The House That Race Built: Black Americans, U.S. Terrain*. Edited by Wahneema Lubiano. New York: Pantheon, 1997. 13–47.

Stenberg, Shari J. "Liberation Theology and Liberatory Pedagogies: Renewing the Dialogue." *College English* 68 (2006): 271–90.

Stephanson, Anders. "Interview with Cornel West." *Social Text* 21 (1989): 269–86.

Stock, Patricia Lambert. *The Dialogic Curriculum: Teaching and Learning in a Multicultural Society*. Portsmouth, NH: Boynton/Cook, 1995.

Stull, Bradford T. *Amid the Fall, Dreaming of Eden: Du Bois, King, Malcolm X, and Emancipatory Composition*. Carbondale: Southern Illinois University Press, 1999.

Symposium Collective. "The Politics of the Personal: Storying Our Lives against the Grain." *College English* 64 (2001): 41–62.

Tan, Amy. "Mother Tongue." In *Rhetorical Choices: A Reader for Writers*. Edited by Keith Gilyard, Deborah H. Holdstein, and Charles I. Schuster. New York: Pearson Longman, 2004. 54–59.

Tannen, Deborah. "Sex, Lies, and Conversation." In *Rhetorical Choices: A Reader for Writers*. Edited by Keith Gilyard, Deborah H. Holdstein, and Charles I. Schuster. New York: Pearson Longman, 2004. 449–54.

———. "What's in a Frame? Surface Evidence for Underlying Expectations." In *New Directions in Discourse Processing*. Edited by R. O. Freedle. Norwood, NJ: Ablex, 1979. 137–81.

Tinberg, Howard B. *Border Talk: Writing and Knowing in the Two-Year College*. Urbana, IL: National Council of Teachers of English, 1997.

Tingle, Nick. "The Vexation of Class." *College English* 67 (2004): 222–30.

Tobin, Jacqueline L., and Raymond G. Dobard. *Hidden in Plain View: A Secret Story of Quilts and the Underground Railroad*. New York: Anchor, 2000.

Trimbur, John. "Composition and the Circulation of Writing." *College Composition and Communication* 52 (2000): 188–219.

Trotsky, Leon. *The New Course*. 1924. Reprint, Ann Arbor: University of Michigan Press, 1975.

Vatz, Richard. "The Myth of the Rhetorical Situation." *Philosophy and Rhetoric* 6 (1973): 154–57.

Vescio, Bryan. Introduction. In *Pragmatism: A New Name for Some Old Ways of Thinking*. By William James. 1907. Reprint, New York: Barnes & Noble, 2003.

Villanueva, Victor, Jr. *Bootstraps: From an American Academic of Color*. Urbana, IL: National Council of Teachers of English, 1993.

Voparil, Christopher J. *Richard Rorty: Politics and Vision*. Lanham, MD: Rowman & Littlefield, 2006.

Walker, Margaret. "Kissie Lee." In *The Riverside Anthology of the African American Literary Tradition*. Edited by Patricia Liggins Hill. Boston: Houghton Mifflin, 1998. 1102–3.

Wallace, David L. "Transcending Normativity: Difference Issues in *College English*." *College English* 68 (2006): 502–30.

Washburn, Jennifer. *University, Inc.: The Corporate Corruption of American Higher Education*. New York: Basic, 2005.

Watkins, S. Craig. *Hip Hop Matters: Politics, Pop Culture, and a Struggle for the Soul of a Movement*. Boston: Beacon, 2005.

Watts, Jerry Gafio. *Heroism and the Black Intellectual: Ralph Ellison, Politics, and Afro-American Intellectual Life*. Chapel Hill: University of North Carolina Press, 1994.

Wells, Harry K. *Pragmatism: Philosophy of Imperialism*. New York: International, 1954.

Werner, Craig. *Higher Ground: Stevie Wonder, Aretha Franklin, Curtis Mayfield, and the Rise and Fall of American Soul*. New York: Three Rivers, 2004.

West, Cornel. *The American Evasion of Philosophy: A Genealogy of Pragmatism*. Madison: University of Wisconsin Press, 1989.

———. "Beyond Affirmative Action: Equality and Identity." In *Race Matters*, Boston: Beacon, 1993. 63–67.

———. "Beyond Multiculturalism and Eurocentrism." In *Beyond Eurocentrism and Multiculturalism. Volume 1, Prophetic Thought in Postmodern Times*. Monroe, ME: Common Courage, 1993. 3–30.

———. *The Cornel West Reader*. New York: Basic *Civitas*, 1999.

———. "The Crisis in Contemporary American Religion." In *Prophetic Fragments: Illuminations of the Crisis in American Religion and Culture*. Grand Rapids, MI: Eerdmans, 1988. ix–xi.

———. *Democracy Matters: Winning the Fight against Imperialism*. New York: Penguin, 2004.

———. *The Ethical Dimensions of Marxist Thought*. New York: Monthly Review, 1991.

———. Foreword. In *Go Down, Moses: Celebrating the African-American Spiritual*. Edited by Richard Newman. New York: Clarkson Potter, 1998. 9–17.

———. "In Memory of Marvin Gaye." In *Prophetic Fragments: Illumina-*

tions of the Crisis in American Religion and Culture. Grand Rapids, MI: Eerdmans, 1988. 174–76.

———. *Keeping Faith: Philosophy and Race in America.* New York: Routledge, 1994.

———. "Martin Luther King Jr.: Prophetic Christian as Organic Intellectual." In *Prophetic Fragments: Illuminations of the Crisis in American Religion and Culture.* Grand Rapids, MI: Eerdmans, 1988. 3–12.

———. "Minority Discourse and the Pitfalls of Canon Formation." *Yale Journal of Criticism* 1 (1987): 193–201.

———. "Nihilism in Black America." In *Race Matters.* Boston: Beacon, 1993. 11–20.

———. "On Afro-American Popular Music: From Bebop to Rap." In *Prophetic Fragments: Illuminations of the Crisis in American Religion and Culture.* Grand Rapids, MI: Eerdmans, 1988. 177–87.

———. "Paulo Freire." In *Beyond Eurocentrism and Multiculturalism. Volume 2, Prophetic Reflections; Notes on Race and Power in America.* Monroe, ME: Common Courage, 1993. 179–80.

———. "Philosophy and the Funk of Life." In *Cornel West: A Critical Reader.* Edited by George Yancy. Malden, MA: Blackwell, 2001. 346–62.

———. *Prophesy Deliverance! An Afro-American Revolutionary Christianity.* 1982. Reprint, Louisville: Westminster John Knox, 2002.

———. *Prophetic Fragments: Illuminations of the Crisis in American Religion and Culture.* Grand Rapids, MI: Eerdmans, 1988.

———. "Prophetic Theology." In *Beyond Eurocentrism and Multiculturalism. Volume 2, Prophetic Reflections; Notes on Race and Power in America.* Monroe, ME: Common Courage, 1993. 223–33.

———. "The Prophetic Tradition in Afro-America." In *Prophetic Fragments: Illuminations of the Crisis in American Religion and Culture.* Grand Rapids, MI: Eerdmans, 1988. 38–49.

———. "Race and Social Theory." In *Keeping Faith: Philosophy and Race in America.* New York: Routledge, 1994. 251–70.

———. *Race Matters.* Boston: Beacon, 1993.

———. "Religion, Politics, Language." In *Prophetic Fragments: Illuminations of the Crisis in American Religion and Culture.* Grand Rapids, MI: Eerdmans, 1998. 22–24.

———. *Sketches of My Culture.* CD. Artemis Records, 2001.

———. "Subversive Joy and Revolutionary Patience in Black Christianity." In *Prophetic Fragments: Illuminations of the Crisis in American Religion and Culture.* Grand Rapids, MI: Eerdmans, 1998. 161–65.

———. "Theory, Pragmatisms, and Politics." In *Keeping Faith: Philosophy and Race in America.* New York: Routledge, 1994. 89–105.

———. "Toward a Socialist Theory of Racism." In *Prophetic Fragments: Illuminations of the Crisis in American Religion and Culture.* Grand Rapids, MI: Eerdmans, 1998. 97–108.

———. "The Tragicomic and the Political in Christian Faith." In *Prophesy Deliverance! An Afro-American Revolutionary Christianity*. 1982. Reprint, Louisville: Westminster John Knox, 2002. 5–10.

———. "A World of Ideas: Interview with Cornel West." By Bill Moyer. In *Beyond Eurocentrism and Multiculturalism. Volume 2, Prophetic Reflections; Notes on Race and Power in America*. Monroe, ME: Common Courage, 1993. 103–12.

West, Kanye. *The College Dropout*. CD. Roc-A-Fella Records, 2004.

———. *Graduation*. CD. Roc-A-Fella Records, 2007.

———. *Late Registration*. CD. Roc-A-Fella Records, 2005.

Williams, Raymond. *Modern Tragedy*. London: Chatto and Windus, 1966.

Wolin, Sheldon S. *The Berkeley Rebellion and Beyond: Essays on Politics and Education in the Technological Society*. New York: Vintage, 1970.

———. "Political Theory as Vocation." *American Political Science Review* 63 (1969): 1062–82.

———. *Politics and Vision: Continuity and Innovation in Western Political Thought*. Boston: Little, Brown, 1960.

———. *Tocqueville between Two Worlds: The Making of a Political and Theoretical Life*. Princeton, NJ: Princeton University Press, 2003.

Wood, Mark David. *Cornel West and the Politics of Prophetic Pragmatism*. Urbana: University of Illinois Press, 2000.

Wright, Richard. *12 Million Black Voices: A Folk History of the Negro in the United States*. 1941. Reprint, New York: Thunder's Mouth, 1988.

Yancy, George. "Cornel West: The Vanguard of Existential and Democratic Hope." In *Cornel West: A Critical Reader*. Edited by George Yancy. Malden, MA: Blackwell, 2001. 1–16.

Young, Morris. *Minor Re/Visions: Asian American Literacy Narratives as a Rhetoric of Citizenship*. Carbondale: Southern Illinois University Press, 2004.

Index

academia, 100, 109, 131n. 3. *See also* education

African American humanism, 23–26

African American Language (AAL), 97

African Americans: academics, 59, 70; and death, 105–6; enslavement of, 80–81; expressive culture of, 25–26, 83–84; folk wisdom of, 64–65; music of, 26, 77–78, 88–98, 104–5, 134–35n. 11 (*see also* spirituals); nihilism of, 65–66, 132–33n. 10; political activity of, 79; response to sojourn in America, 23–24; students, 33–34, 46–47, 130n. 4

"Ain't No Way" (Robinson), 86

Alim, H. Samy, 98

Alinsky, Saul, 111–12

Allen, Theodore, 63

"Amen" (Mayfield), 79

American Evasion of Philosophy, The (West), 8, 25–26, 60

"Ante-Bellum Sermon" (Dunbar), 81

antifoundationalism, 55

Apology (Plato), 123–24n. 2

assimilationism, 23

autoethnography, 66–67

Baraka, Amiri, 91

Be (Common), 91

Beech, Jennifer, 69

Berg, Paul, 100

Bernstein, Basil, 33

Bernstein, Eduard, 18

Berthoff, Ann, 54–55, 129n. 1

Bitzer, Lloyd, 64–65

Bizzell, Patricia, 101

Black Arts Movement, 23, 78

Blackman, Toni, 93–94

Black Power Movement, 24, 78, 82, 85, 87

blue-collar class, 68

blues sensibility, 26, 77, 90, 133–34n. 1

Bluest Eye, The (Morrison), 28

Branch, Margaret, 87

Branch, Taylor, 129n. 14

Brown, James, 78

Bryant, Brenda, 87

Butler, Octavia, 92

Bynoe, Yvonne, 95

Campbell, JoAnn, 54–55

capitalism, 30, 61–63

Capriccio (Strauss), 102

Carmichael, Stokely, 128–29n. 13

Cartesian rationalism, 8

CCCC. *See* Conference on College Composition and Communication (CCCC)

Chavez, Hugo, 117

"Choice of Colors" (Mayfield), 84

Christian fundamentalism, 21, 56

Christianity, prophetic, 19–23, 60

"Christmas Sermon on Peace" (King), 54
Chuck D (rap artist), 90, 134–35n. 11
citizenship training, 116
Civil Rights Movement, music and, 78–79, 84–85, 87, 96. *See also individual artists*
civil society, 127–28n. 12
Clark, Romy, 17–18
class matters, 13, 67–71, 114–15
CNN, 98, 134–35n. 11
College Dropout, The (K. West), 95
college students. *See* students
Coltrane, John, 104
combative spirituality, 58–59
Common (rap artist), 91
Communist Manifesto, The (Marx and Engels), 127n. 9
community, inquiring, 7–8
community of origin, 129n. 13
composition and compositionists: African American, 59; critical, and prophetic witness, 52; emancipatory, 3; Gramsci's influence on, 17–18; pragmatism and, 106–7; radical, and Christian theorists, 58; rap music and, 98; and Socratic commitment, 100–101
composition studies: and class, 69–70; and conceptions of language, 106; and deep democracy, 99; first-year writing courses, 4; and politics, 28–29; and religion, 56–57
Cone, James, 133–34n. 1
Conference on College Composition and Communication (CCCC), 2, 41, 70–71
conservatism, 29–30, 32
Constantinian Christianity, 60
Cooke, Sam, 78
councilism, 18
Cowan, Rosemary, 22, 77–78
critical composition, 52
critical intelligence, 108–9
critical literacy, 27–34, 50, 101
critical pedagogy, 58, 61–62, 116–17
Crowley, Sharon, 131–32n. 3
"Crying of Water, The" (Symons), 108
cultural codes, 72

cultural criticism, 13, 85–86
cultural debates, 96–97

Daniell, Beth, 54–55
Dantley, Michael, 61–62
Dead Prez (rap group), 92–93
deep democracy, 3, 99, 112–13
Delta Meets Detroit (Franklin), 86–87
democracies: American, 59–63; creative, 39; deep, 3, 99, 112–13; majority tyranny vs., 48
Democracy Matters (West), 4–5, 19, 60, 123n. 2
Derrida, Jacques, 74–75
Descartes, René, 62–63
Dewey, John, 8–10, 107–8, 125n. 2 (chap. 1)
discourse: in composition, 131–32n. 3; proposed strategies, 5; public, quality of, 101; religious, 60; student understanding of, 29–30; white supremacist, 62–63
discursivity, 73
disidentification, 43–44
Dobard, Raymond G., 80
Dobkin, Matt, 85
double-consciousness, 11–12
double-voiced rhetorical strategies, 83–85
Dowd, Tom, 84
Du Bois, W. E. B., 3, 11–12, 23, 91–92, 108–9
Dunbar, Paul L., 81
Durst, Russell K., 55
Dyson, Michael Eric, 87

Ebonics, 32–34, 132n. 7
education, 10, 27–28, 100–101, 115–16, 130n. 4. *See also* composition studies; critical pedagogy; rhetorical education
educators, progressive, 57
Ellison, Ralph, 24–25, 129n. 16
Emerson, Ralph Waldo, 8–9, 12, 126n. 3
Enlightenment philosophers, 63. *See also individual philosophers*
ethnographies, 42–43, 57, 66–67
Evers, Medgar, 79
exceptionalism, 23–24
exnomination, idea of, 30

faith matters, 52–53, 55–59, 110–11
"Fine Old Firm, A" (Jackson), 34–39
first-year writing courses, 4
Fishman, Andrea, 43
Fishman, Stephen M., 10
Flavor Flav (rap artist), 90
Flower, Linda, 49–50, 106
"Flyin' High" (Gaye), 87
folk wisdom, 64–65
"Fool for You" (Mayfield), 83–84, 86
Foucault, Michel, 71–76, 124n. 2, 133n.
    11–12
"Fourth Branch, The" (Immortal Tech-
    nique), 93
frames, concept of, 30
Franklin, Aretha, 78, 84–87
Frazier, E. Franklin, 23
freedom, in prophetic Christianity, 20
Freire, Paulo, 27–28, 54, 58, 110–12
fundamentalism, 21, 56, 58, 61

Galloway, A. Scott, 134n. 5
Gaye, Marvin, 78, 87–88
George, Robert, 117
Gere, Anne Ruggles, 55–56
Gilles, Roger, 106
Gilyard, Keith: courses taught by, 29–30,
    39; Cornel West interview, 101–19
Giroux, Henry, 4, 28, 129n. 1
Giroux, Susan Searls, 4
Glaude, Eddie S., Jr., 135n. 6
Goodburn, Amy, 56
Gordy, Berry, 87
"Gospel Train, The" (spiritual), 82
Grae, Jean, 93–95
grammatical errors, 31–32
Gramsci, Antonio, 17–18, 93, 127n. 12
Guinier, Lani, 46–49

Habermas, Jürgen, 74–75
Hahn, Nance, 41, 44
Hairston, Maxine, 29
Hall, Stuart, 62
"Hard Knock Life" (Jay-Z), 90
Harlem Renaissance, 23
hegemony, defined, 128n. 12
Hidden in Plain View (Tobin and Dobard),
    80
Higgins, Lorraine, 49–50

Hill, Lauryn, 92
hip-hop, 88–98, 134–35n. 11
Hip-Hop Matters (Watkins), 89–90
Hobbes, Thomas, 15, 127n. 8
Hook, Sidney, 126n. 4
Hooker, John Lee, 90
hooks, bell, 53, 110, 115
Horace, 103
Horton, Myles, 111–12, 135n. 6
Hughes, Langston, 39–41
Hugo, Victor, 105
humanism, 23–26
human voice, power of, 102–3
Hume, David, 63
Hurlbert, Claude, 70–71

identity, 40–41, 53, 104
identity politics, 68
"I Have a Dream" (King), 54, 83, 130–31n.
    2 (chap. 3)
Immortal Technique (rap artist), 92–95
imperialism, 60–63
"Inner City Blues" (Gaye), 88
intellectual force, 127n. 11
intellectuals, 58, 128n. 13
Islamic fundamentalism, 61
Ivanič, Roz, 17–18

Jackson, Shirley, 34–39
James, William, 8–9, 125–26n. 2 (chap. 2)
Jay-Z (rap artist), 90
jazz, 26
Jefferson, Thomas, 63
Johnson, James W., 79–80
"Journey, The" (West), 78
Joyce, James, 91–92

kairos, 64
Kant, Immanuel, 63
"Keep on Pushing" (Mayfield), 79
King, Martin Luther, Jr.: and African
    American political activity, 79; and
    democratic ideals, 61; and excep-
    tionalism, 23; and Aretha Franklin,
    85; and humanism, 24; influence of,
    87; and nonviolence, 129n. 15; Stull
    on, 3; West on, 21; works by, 54, 83,
    130–31n. 2 (chap. 3); on world per-
    spective, 130n. 1

Kirsch, Gesa, 55
Korsch, Karl, 18
KRS-One, 90
Kweli, Talib, 91–94

labor movement, 68
Lakoff, Robin, 30, 46
language: African American, 97; and composition pedagogy, 106; conservative ideology of, 32; of critique, 56 (*see also* critical pedagogy); Ebonics, 32–34, 132n. 7; of enslavement, 80–81; ethnographic studies of, 42–43; and habit formation, 45–46; lack of neutrality in, 36–37; of liberation, 27, 80; metaawareness about, 3; right to one's own, 70; Standardized English, 64; West on models for, 74–75
Lanier-Nabors, Benjamin G., 69
Last Poets, The, 91
Lattimore, Almeda, 87
Lazere, Donald, 28–29
Leninism, 17
Leopardi, Giacomo, 107–8
"Letter from Birmingham City Jail" (King), 54
Liang, Sunny, 30–32
liberation theology, 22, 117
Lindquist, Julie, 67–68
linguistic theory, Ebonics and, 33
linguistic therapy, 64
Linkon, Sherry Lee, 69
literacy: autobiographies of, 41–42, 44–46; critical, 27–34, 50, 101
Long, Elenore, 49–50
Lott, Eric, 66, 132–33n. 10
Lu, Min-Zhan, 55
Luxemburg, Rosa, 18

M-1 (rap artist), 92–93
Madhubuti, Haki, 92
Mailer, Norman, 91–92
Mailloux, Steven, 14, 126n. 6
majority rule as tyranny, 46–49
Malcolm X, 3, 23, 87, 93
Marable, Manning, 89–90
Marback, Richard, 65–66, 132n. 7
Marcuse, Herbert, 64
marginalism, 23

Marxism, 14–19
material force, 127n. 11
Matthews, Victoria Earle, 65
Mayfield, Curtis, 78–79, 81–84, 86, 88–89, 98
McCarthy, Lucille, 10
McClaren, Peter L., 61–62
McCrary, Donald, 59
MC Lyte (rap artist), 93
media: corporate, 93; and Liang e-mail, 31–32; liberal bias of, 29–31, 33–34; role and responsibility of, 28
"Meeting Over Yonder" (Mayfield), 79
Melle Mel (rap artist), 90
"Mercy Mercy Me" (Gaye), 88
middle class, 68–69
Miller, Keith D., 83
Mills, C. Wright, 12
"mind's sweet shipwreck," 108–9
Moffett, James, 23, 54–55
moralistic acts vs. moral actions, 21
Moral Majority, 21
Morgan, Marcyliena, 97–98
Morrison, Toni, 28, 99
"Ms. Hill" (Kweli), 92
Muhammad, Elijah, 23
Mumia Abu-Jamal, 93

new positivism, 55
New University Conference, 70
New York Post, 30–32
Niebuhr, Reinhold, 9, 126n. 4
Nietzsche, Friedrich, 103
normative gaze, 63
norms, discursive power of, 30
"No Thing on Me (Cocaine Song)" (Mayfield), 88

Odyssey Project, 41–49, 99
Ohmann, Richard, 126–27n. 7
Olney, James, 41–42
"On the Passing of the First-Born" (Du Bois), 108–9
O'Reilly, Bill, fans of, 34
organic intellectuals, 128n. 13
Owens, Derek, 70–71

paideia concept, 102, 124–25n. 2
Pan Africanism, 129n. 13

Pannekoek, Anton, 18
Pari, Caroline, 129n. 1
Parks, Stephen, 69–70
parrhesia, 123–25n. 2
Peckham, Irvin, 69
Pedagogy of the Oppressed (Freire), 27
Peirce, Charles Sanders, 8–9, 125–26n. 2 (chap. 2)
"People Get Ready" (Mayfield), 79, 82
Perkins, Priscilla, 56–57
Perry, Imani, 134n. 6
Perry, William C., Jr., 101
Phelps, Louise W., 41
philosophy and philosophers, 63, 102–3, 105, 107–8. *See also individual philosophers*
Plato, 50–51, 101–2, 123–24n. 2
Plvan, Faith, 41, 43–44
poets of soul, 78–88
political action, 13
political society, 127–28n. 12
political theology, 22
politics in the composition classroom, 28–29
Poovey, Mary, 85–86
positivism: new, 55; and race matters, 62–63
Pough, Gwendolyn, 98
"Poverty of Philosophy, The" (Immortal Technique), 93
power: concept of, 72–75; desire for, 127n. 8; of human voice, 102–3; of norms, 30; state coercive, 128n. 12; teaching and, 72–75. *See also* Black Power Movement
Power (Foucault), 133n. 11
pragmatism: activism and, 11; and class, 13; composition practices and, 106–7; inauguration of, 9; principle of, 125–26n. 2 (chap. 2); prophetic witness in, 26; rhetorical, 126n. 6; tenets of, 8; weaknesses of, 12–13. *See also* prophetic pragmatism
pragmatist inquiry, 13
preachers and preaching, 103–4
Prescott Elementary School (Oakland, California), 33
"Prophecy, The" (Immortal Technique), 93

Prophesy Deliverance! (West), 13, 20, 23–24, 26, 62–63
prophetic activity, features of, 21
prophetic Christianity, 19–23, 60
prophetic church, 55
prophetic pragmatism, 6, 13–14, 49, 109–10
prophetic tradition, 58–59
prophetic witness, 5, 21–22, 26, 52
Public Enemy, 134–35n. 11
"Pusherman" (Mayfield), 88

Queen Latifah, 90

Rabinow, Paul, 76
race matters, 61–64, 70–71, 113–14
Race Matters (West), 65–67, 113
racism, conceptions of, 63
radio stations, black-oriented, 83
Rand, Lizabeth A., 57–58
rap artists, female, 93, 134n. 6
rap music, 88–98, 134–35n. 11
Ratcliffe, Krista, 65–67
Rawls, John, 60
RBG (Revolutionary but Gangsta) Code, 92
Redding, Otis, 84–86
regimes of truth, 72
religion, 52–53, 55–59, 110–11
Religious Right, 21, 60
"Respect" (Redding), 84–86
Revolutionary but Gangsta (Dead Prez), 92
rhetorical education: and deep democracy, 99; and democratic experimentation, 4; faith issues in, 52, 110–11; race matters in, 62; use of term, 3; value of, 101; West and, 6, 106
rhetorical listening, 66–67
rhetorical positions, unmarked, 30, 46
rhetorical pragmatism, 126n. 6
rhetorical situations, 64–65
Richardson, Elaine, 98
rival hypothesis stance (RHS), 49–50
rivaling, defined, 49–50
Robeson, Paul, 25, 129n. 17
Ronald, Kate, 10–11, 106
Rorty, Richard, 9, 60–61, 126n. 4
Roskelly, Hephzibah, 10–11, 106

Rousseau, Jean-Jacques, 15
Royer, Daniel J., 106
Russell, Bertrand, 50
Rustin, Bayard, 24

Sanjek, Rojer, 63
"Save the Children" (Gaye), 87–88
Schneider, Stephen, 128n. 13
Selsam, Harry, 14
"Share Your Love with Me" (Malone, Braggs), 86
Shor, Ira, 129n. 1
"Sites of Spiritual Composing" (Berthoff et al.), 54–55
Smitherman, Geneva, 96–97
social class, 68–69
socialism, 30
socialist rappers, 92–93
Socratic commitment, 5, 26, 100–101
Socratic commitment *plus,* 49–50
Socratic dialogue, 28, 50, 112–13, 125n. 2 (chap. 1)
soul, spoken, 64
soul artists, 78–88. *See also individual artists*
Souls of Black Folk, The (Du Bois), 108
Southern Christian Leadership Conference, 85
spirituality, 53, 58–59
spirituals, 79–81, 90, 107–8, 133–34n. 1
Stalinism, 17
Standardized English, 64
"Steal Away to Jesus" (spiritual), 80
Steele, Claude M., 43–44, 130n. 4
Steinberg, Michael, 104
Steinberg, Stephen, 65–66
Stenberg, Shari J., 58
Stephanson, Anders, 74–75
Stic.Man (rap artist), 92–93
Stix, Nicholas, 130n. 3
Stock, Patricia, 41
Stout, Jeff, 117–18
students: African American, 33–34, 46–47, 130n. 4; *The College Dropout,* 95; on media bias, 29–32; and Odyssey Project, 43; and religion, 53, 55, 57; response to "A Fine Old Firm," 34–39; view of composition instructors, 68–69

"Students' Right to Their Own Language" resolution, 70
Stull, Bradford T., 3, 53–54
subjectivities, and race, 62
subjects, as constituted vs. dynamic practices, 73–74
Superfly (Mayfield), 88–89, 98
Superfly (movie), 134n. 5
Swearingen, C. Jan, 54–55
Symons, Arthur, 108

teaching, as exercise in power, 72–75
"Theme for English B" (Hughes), 39–41
"There's No Hiding Place Down There" (spiritual), 82
"Think" (Franklin), 86
"This Is My Country" (Mayfield), 83–84
Till, Emmett, 81–82
Tingle, Nick, 69
Tobin, Jacqueline L., 80
"Toward a Socialist Theory of Racism" (West), 63
tragicomic hope, 5–6, 23–26, 77–78
transformative intellectual vs. prophetic teacher, 58
Trimbur, John, 15–17
Trotskyism, 17
truth, regimes of, 72

union organizers, 129n. 13
unmarked rhetorical position, 30, 46

Vandross, Luther, 78
Vatz, Richard, 65
Vaughn, Sarah, 104
Vescio, Bryan, 125n. 2 (chap. 2)
Villaneuva, Victor, Jr., 17
vocation and invocation, 119
voting, 47–48

Walker, Margaret, 134n. 6
Walker, Wyatt T., 24
Wallace, David L., 55–56, 131n. 3
Washburn, Jennifer, 100
Washington Times, 32–34
Watkins, Craig S., 89–90, 96
Watts, Jerry, 129n. 16

Wells, Harry K., 14
"We're a Winner" (Mayfield), 82–83
"We're Rolling On" (Mayfield), 83
Werner, Craig, 82
West, Cornel: and African American music, 78; on battle for democracy, 59–60; on black cultural output and life, 25–26; courses and seminars of, 117–18; on culture of creative democracy, 39; discursive strategies proposed by, 5; Flower on, 49; on Foucault and agency, 74; Foucault compared to, 75–76; on Paulo Freire, 28; Gilyard interview of, 101–19; on hip-hop, 89; impact of, on scholars, 2; on language models, 74–75; on pragmatism within Western philosophical tradition, 107; on prophetic witness, 52; on race matters, 61–64; and rhetorical education, 6; on Socratic questioning, 50; taxonomy of, 127n. 10; themes of, 7; on the tragicomic, 77; on white-dominated political movements, 71. *See also individual titles*

West, Kanye, 95
Wexler, Jerry, 84
What's Going On (Gaye), 87–88
"What's Happening Brother" (Gaye), 87
white-collar class, 68
white supremacy, 62–65, 114–17
Williams, Raymond, 25
Wolin, Sheldon, 118–19
womanist theology, 59
Wood, Mark David, 14, 19, 75
working class, 68–69
Wright, Richard, 25, 129n. 17
writing courses, first-year, 4
writing studios, 42

Yagelski, Robert, 70–71
Yancey, Kathleen, 40–41
Yancy, George, 77, 119
Young, Morris, 65, 67

KEITH GILYARD is Distinguished Professor of English at the Pennsylvania State University, where he teaches courses in composition, rhetorical theory, and literature. His books include *Voices of the Self: A Study of Language Competence*, for which he won an American Book Award; *Let's Flip the Script: An African American Discourse on Language, Literature, and Learning*; and *Liberation Memories: The Rhetoric and Poetics of John Oliver Killens*. In 2000, he served as chair of the Conference on College Composition and Communication.